School-Based Enterprise

David Stern
James Stone III
Charles Hopkins
Martin McMillion
Robert Crain

School-Based Enterprise

Productive Learning in American High Schools

Jossey-Bass Publishers · San Francisco

Substantial discounts on bulk quantities of Jossey-Bass books are available to corporations, professional associations, and other organizations. For details and discount information, contact the special sales department at Jossey-Bass Inc., Publishers. (415) 433-1740; Fax (415) 433-0499.

Manufactured in the United States of America. Nearly all Jossey-Bass books and jackets are printed on recycled paper containing at least 10 percent postconsumer waste, and many are printed with either soy- or vegetable-based ink, which emits fewer volatile organic compounds during the printing process than petroleum-based ink.

Library of Congress Cataloging-in-Publication Data

School-based enterprise : productive learning in American high schools
  / David Stern . . . [et al.].
      p.   cm. — (Jossey-Bass education series)
  Includes bibliographical references and index.
  ISBN 1-55542-597-6
    1. Education, Secondary — Economic aspects — United States.
  2. Distributive education — United States.   3. Career education —
  United States.   4. Vocational education — United States.
  5. Education, Secondary — Social aspects — United States.   I. Stern,
  David, date.   II. Series.
  LC67.52.S37 1993
  370.11′3 — dc20   93-29489
                                                                  CIP

FIRST EDITION
HB Printing   10 9 8 7 6 5 4 3 2

THE JOSSEY-BASS
EDUCATION SERIES

CONTENTS

**Part Four: The Future
of School-Based Enterprise**

9.   A Strategy for Expansion   204

     References   211

     Index   215

PREFACE

SCHOOL-BASED ENTERPRISE (SBE) SHOULD BE CONSIDERED AS A possible means to accomplish the two main missions of American high schools: preparing students for work and for further education. Students in thousands of high schools every year perform substantial productive activities that add to their academic and vocational preparation. They build or rehabilitate houses, staff child-care centers, publish books or magazines, run restaurants, raise crops or livestock, fix cars, operate retail outlets, and provide other services as part of their school programs. But the existence and potential significance of these activities have, for the most part, been overlooked. This book calls attention to school-based enterprise and explains its possible importance.

School-based enterprise can be defined as any school-sponsored activity that engages a group of students in producing goods or services for sale to or use by people other than the students involved. These enterprise activities are sometimes found at the high school level, and they are common practice in postgraduate education; for example, law students publish law review journals and doctoral students produce new research. SBEs have usually been confined to vocational and professional education, however. Despite some notable exceptions, they have rarely appeared in conjunction with high school English, math, science, social studies, or other nonvocational courses. This is unfortunate, because the potential advantages of school-based enterprise transcend preparation for specific kinds of work. These advantages include deeper understanding of academic subject matter through application in a practical context, motivation that comes from solving problems with immediate consequences, and generic work skills (such as collaborating in teams and knowing how to use work as a learning experience). With recent research in cognitive science creating renewed interest in methods of active and cooperative learning, there should be greater appreciation for the particular advantages of school-based enterprise.

In addition to educational outcomes, school-based enterprise can produce material benefits. Revenues from some enterprises help pay expenses for schools and students. Some SBEs benefit consumers or clients by providing goods or services at less than the market price. Some SBEs spin off businesses or business ideas that contribute to local economic development. Perhaps most important in the long run, SBEs serve as laboratories to test new methods for organizing productive activity to promote learning — methods that may have great value for nonschool business enterprises striving to become "learning organizations."

SBEs also appear to yield nonpecuniary benefits to people other than the participating students. These result from cultivation of students' commitment to high standards of quality at work, increased student interest in community service, and the encouragement that participating students receive to complete high school.

Intent of the Book

This book contains concrete illustrations of these apparent educational, economic, and social benefits, drawn from observations and interviews with students and faculty members in SBEs at sixteen sites. In legal parlance, we are at the stage of showing probable cause, not proving beyond a reasonable doubt. We seek a warrant for systematic analysis and evaluation of school-based enterprise by educators and researchers. Most of the evidence we present here is in the words of students, teachers, and administrators from recorded interviews, altered only to correct the occasional solecisms that occur in ordinary speech but look bad in print.

We have written this book primarily for administrators

and teachers, especially at the secondary level, who are searching for ideas to make school more effective by making it more real. (That is one reason why we have presented so many of the ideas in the words of teachers and administrators themselves.) In addition, we think this book should be of interest to researchers and policy makers, including school board members, who are concerned with secondary education. The question of how best to relate school and work is both timely and timeless. Can high schools prepare students for work and college at the same time, without resort to invidious forms of tracking? School-based enterprise provides a distinctive and potentially powerful answer.

Overview of the Contents

The idea of school-based enterprise is not new. In Chapter One, we briefly review some of the sources and outline the educational, economic, and social purposes for which school-based enterprise has been proposed. We also provide evidence from a small sample of students who participate both in SBEs and in outside jobs not supervised by the school. The students' responses indicate that they feel the SBE experience contributes more to their education. However, granted that school-based enterprise has more educational content than outside jobs, this evidence says nothing about whether it adds educational value to regular classroom activities. That is the subject of Chapters Three through Five.

Before presenting evidence from the case studies, we describe the sixteen case study sites in Chapter Two. These brief descriptions are intended to form an image of each SBE in the reader's mind, so that the programs will be recognizable when they are mentioned in subsequent chapters. The descriptions also illustrate the range of contexts in which SBEs occur: comprehensive high schools, vocational secondary schools, and programs for selected student populations ranging from the academically gifted to wards of the court. We also include two community colleges, to indicate the possibilities there.

Chapter Three documents how the sixteen SBEs we studied address themselves to educational purposes. In these enterprises, students strengthen their grasp of material from academic and vocational courses; they encounter many aspects of an industry and confront a range of problems; they practice teamwork; and they have a chance to learn specific and generic work skills, including how to use work itself as a learning experience. Students also participate in designing and redesigning their own work organizations.

The economic and social benefits of school-based enterprise are described in Chapters Four and Five. In the American political economy, school-based enterprise would normally be considered appropriate if the educational benefits to students combined with the benefits to other people were worth more than the total cost of the activity and if it would not be feasible for a profit-seeking business to provide the product or service. These considerations define a niche for school-based enterprise that includes one set of activities producing spillover benefits and another set consisting of labor-intensive enterprises. Chapter Four describes how the SBEs we studied realize the economic benefits of cost recovery, providing goods or services at less than market price, and contributing to community economic development. It also indicates some of the potential for SBEs to serve as workplace laboratories, developing methods of organization that can improve practice in nonschool enterprises.

In Chapter Five, we present findings about social benefits. In most of our study sites, SBE teachers expressed a desire for students to understand the importance of high standards for quality, and at least some students are getting the message. Some SBEs affirm the value of community service as well. Retaining students who might otherwise drop out of high school is also seen as an outcome of some SBEs.

If SBEs can provide all these benefits, why is school-based enterprise not a more central part of the high school curriculum? (Although thousands of high schools sponsor SBEs, they are usually marginal programs involving only a few dozen students for a few hours a week.) Chapters Six and Seven shed some light on this question. In Chapter Six, we describe the complex package of resources and conditions necessary for starting a school enterprise. In light of that burden, it is not surprising that most high school SBEs are limited to single classes, usually in vocational subjects. Only a few attempt the more ambitious task of bringing in students from different classes. Chapter Seven considers some of the difficulties that arise in running a school enterprise after it is under way. Getting students to take initiative, organizing the curriculum, structuring incentives for students, maintaining support networks and partnerships, and meeting production schedules while giving students plenty of time to learn—these are some of the ongoing challenges in any SBE. Even a high school teacher or administrator convinced of the value of school-based enterprise would hesitate to take on these challenges without additional support.

In Chapter Eight, we propose a vision of what high school might be like if school-based enterprise played a central part. We create two fictitious high schools, one urban and one exurban. They are collages composed mainly of things that we have seen but also including elements that we have only imagined. They are intended to suggest how SBEs might enable high school students both to advance themselves and to serve their communities. Then, in Chapter Nine, we outline elements of a strategy to implement this vision in U.S. high schools. Components of the strategy include a new view of education and work, an investment in teachers and curriculum, a set of flexible administrative arrangements, and a rigorous procedure for ongoing evaluation. We offer this as an agenda for ourselves and others.

The research for this book was supported by the U.S. Department of Education through a grant to the National Center for Research in Vocational Education at the University of California, Berkeley. Our conclusions do not necessarily represent official U.S. Department of Education positions or policy.

To conduct the fieldwork, we went in teams (usually two but sometimes more) to each site for at least two days, conducting semistructured interviews and observations. James Stone took the lead in coordinating the fieldwork. David Stern took major responsibility for writing the book, using field notes and drafts of some sections produced by all team members. James Stone created the scenarios in Chapter Eight.

We are grateful to everyone at the sixteen case study sites who took time to help us with this research. We were repeatedly impressed by the ingenuity and commitment of teachers and administrators. Our hope is that this book provides a suitable vehicle for them to speak for themselves.

November 1993

David Stern
Berkeley, California

James Stone III
St. Paul, Minnesota

Charles Hopkins
St. Paul, Minnesota

Martin McMillion
Blacksburg, Virginia

Robert Crain
New York, New York

THE AUTHORS

DAVID STERN is professor of education at the University of California, Berkeley. He received his A.B. degree (1966) from Harvard University in social relations, his M.S. degree (1968) from the Massachusetts Institute of Technology (MIT) in city planning, and his Ph.D. degree (1972) from MIT in economics and urban studies.

His primary research activities have been in the economics of education — including efficiency and equity in the allocation of school resources and connections between schooling and labor markets. In recent years, his main interest has been in how learning and work complement or conflict with each other both for working students and for employed adults. His books include *Managing Human Resources: The Art of Full Employment* (1982), *Adolescence and Work: Influences of Social Structure, Labor Markets, and Culture* (1989, coedited with D. Eichorn), *Market Failure in Training? New Economic Analysis and Evidence on Training of Adult Employees* (1991, coedited with J. Ritzen), and *Career Academies: Partnerships for Reconstructing American High Schools* (1992, with M. Raby and C. Dayton).

JAMES STONE III is associate professor of vocational education at the University of Minnesota. After a decade in retail management, he received his B.S. degree (1976) from Virginia Polytechnic Institute and State University in education, his M.S. degree (1980) from George Mason University in education, and his Ed.D. degree (1983) from Virginia Polytechnic Institute and State University.

Stone advises schools and community organizations on the development of youth employment and training programs. His main research activities have been in education and work transitions for adolescents and adults and in vocational education for business careers. He has twice received the Neil Vivian Research Award from the American Vocational Association (1984 and 1987) and three times been recognized as presenting the Outstanding Research Paper by the American Vocational Education Research Association (1985, 1987, 1988). In addition to more than thirty journal articles, Stone has authored two texts for secondary classroom use: *Retail Marketing: Principles and Practices* (1988, with others) and *Marketing: A Customer Service Approach* (forthcoming).

CHARLES HOPKINS is professor of business and marketing education in the College of Education at the University of Minnesota. He received his B.S. degree (1960) from St. Cloud State University in business education, his M.A. degree (1966) from the University of Minnesota in curriculum and instruction, and his Ph.D. degree (1968) in education, also from the University of Minnesota.

Hopkins's main research activities have been in basic business and economics education and the study of programs designed to improve the transition from school to work for secondary and technical/community college students. He directed several state-funded curriculum development projects that helped Minnesota Technical Colleges restructure and update their business and marketing curricula. He has served as acting executive director of the Minnesota Council on Economic Education. Hopkins was coauthor of *General Business in Our Modern Society* (1979, with others); in addition, he has authored or coauthored more than eighty articles, chapters, and research reports related to his research interests.

MARTIN McMILLION is associate professor of agricultural education at Virginia Polytechnic Institute and State University. He received his B.S. degree (1954) from West Virginia University in agricultural education, his M.Ed. degree (1959) from Pennsylvania State University in agricultural education, and his Ed.D. degree (1966) from the University of Illinois in education.

McMillion's research activities have centered on experiential education and adult education. He has studied the operation of school farms in Brazil, Panama, New Zealand, Australia, and the United States and was a Fulbright Research Scholar to New Zealand in 1960. He was associated with the National Center for Research in Vocational Education from 1988 to 1993, researching school-directed work experience and school-based enterprises, and has been editor of *Agricultural Education Magazine.*

ROBERT CRAIN is a professor at Teachers College, Columbia University, where he heads the programs in Sociology and Education and Politics and Education. He earned a B.A. degree (1956) from the University of Louisville in mathematics and engineering; his Ph.D. degree (1963) is from the University of Chicago in sociology. He taught sociology there and at Johns Hopkins University and was with the Rand Corporation in its Santa Monica, California, and Washington, D.C., offices. Most of his research has been in evaluation of educational programs, studies of school social climates, school desegregation, and race relations. Three of his books are *The Politics of School Desegregation* (1969, with M. Inger, G. A. McWorter, and J. J. Vanecko), *Discrimination, Personality, and Achievement: A Survey of Northern Blacks* (1972, with C. S. Weisman), and *Making Desegregation Work: How Schools Create Social Climates* (1982, with R. E. Mahard and R. E. Narot).

School-Based Enterprise

PART ONE

School-Based Enterprise and American High Schools

1

The Idea of
Learning by Producing

*L*et us consider school-based enterprise (SBE) as a strategy to prepare high school students for college or work. We can define school-based enterprise as any activity through which students produce goods or services for sale to or use by people other than themselves. For example, high school students build or rehabilitate houses, staff child-care centers, fix cars, run restaurants, raise crops or livestock, and create clothing. Students restore historic landmarks, conduct research on local environmental quality, engage in small-scale manufacturing, and perform other productive services. Such activities can provide some of the same work-preparation advantages as employer-based apprenticeship. They can also yield the academic benefits that have been claimed for cognitive apprenticeship as a general model of learning.

Both work-based apprenticeship and cognitive apprenticeship have been the subject of much recent discussion. The aim of work-based "youth apprenticeship" is to improve high school students' career preparation by giving students two or three years of structured, work-based learning linked to classroom instruction, leading to a recognized certificate that qualifies them for employment. But youth apprenticeship can become an option for a significant number of students only if enough employers make the necessary arrangements to accommodate young trainees. To create apprenticeships for 15 percent of the age group between sixteen and twenty, one of every five U.S. employers would have to offer at least one slot (Olson, 1993a). Whether this will occur is uncertain (Bailey, 1993).

Apprenticeship is also being proposed as a general model of learning that can improve instruction in academic subjects and therefore serve both students who plan to attend college and those who plan to work full-time after completing high school (Berryman, 1992; Resnick, 1987a, 1987b; Raizen, 1989; Brown, Collins, and Duguid, 1989). In contrast to the passive learning typical of many high school classrooms, cognitive apprenticeship engages students in active problem solving. Instead of fragmenting knowledge into the unrelated subjects of the conventional curriculum, cognitive apprenticeship gives students whole tasks that require integration of knowledge from various disciplines. As opposed to presenting facts and procedures outside their contexts of use, cognitive apprenticeship places learning in a practical context where students can find meaning. For these reasons, information and thought processes acquired through cognitive apprenticeship are more likely to be remembered and available for application to future problems. This approach has been advocated by the National Council of Teachers of Mathematics (1989), among other groups.

Yet just as work-based apprenticeship requires employers to provide training slots, cognitive apprenticeship requires teachers to create learning situations for students that are active, integrated, and real. Most teachers are not doing that now. The fact that virtually all the design teams selected to develop "break-the-mold" schools for the New American Schools Development Corporation have emphasized "project learning" similar to cognitive apprenticeship indicates both the theoretical appeal of this model and its scarcity in current practice (Olson, 1993b).

School-based enterprise could be designed to prepare students for both college and work. In a house-building project, for example, students could acquire construction skills and also work out the mathematics of structural forces. Students in a school restaurant could make soups and sauces as well as analyze their nutritional content. Students running a child-care center could learn how to organize games for three-year-olds in addition to theories of child development.

In spite of their potential, SBEs are one of the best-kept secrets in American education, scarcely mentioned in discussions of policy for educational reform. Until recently, no one had even tried to count how many SBEs there are. But a 1992 national survey of public secondary schools discovered that 18.6 percent were sponsoring at least one SBE, defined in the survey as "a class-related activity that engages students in producing goods or services for sale or use to people other than the participating students themselves" (Stern, 1992b). In this book, we describe sixteen examples illustrating a range of actual applications in American high schools.

Origins and Purposes of SBE

The idea of school-based enterprise is not new. The practical possibility of generating revenues to offset the cost of schooling has appealed to many people. According to von Borstel's (1982) historical review of the concept of productive education, one of the earliest proponents was the English political philosopher John Locke. In his 1696 *Plan for Working-Schools for Poor Children*, Locke envisioned an institution that would train and care for indigent children, supported by the work of the children themselves. Self-sufficiency through sale of goods produced by the schools was a salient feature of the plan. Von Borstel finds a similar idea later in the English socialist Robert Owen's 1818 *Report to the Committee of the Association for the Relief of the Poor.* Owen applied the idea of productive education in the community he founded at New Lanark. A more recent application of the same concept was the Supported Work Demonstration in the United States during the 1970s, which created enterprises for the purpose of training welfare recipients, former drug addicts, unemployed youth, and former prison inmates (Manpower Demonstration Research Corporation, 1980).

Von Borstel credits the Russian educator Anton Semenovitch Makarenko with the first actual demonstration of cost recovery through school enterprise. At the Gorky Colony during the 1920s and 1930s, students operated a number of successful enterprises, starting with the farming of grain, vegetables, fruit, and livestock and eventually including the manufacture of clothing, furniture, and cameras. These enterprises were able to generate profits with students working four hours a day and devoting the rest of their time to studies.

Cost recovery tends to be a more important objective for SBEs in situations where resource scarcity is more pressing. Developing countries, for example, often use SBEs. Von Borstel's survey of twenty-seven productive education projects in developing countries found that nine of them generated enough revenue to pay all the costs of the school, another five supported between 60 and 90 percent of school costs, and six more recovered between 25 and 45 percent. This implies that the enterprises produced enough not only to cover the cost of production itself but also, in many instances, to cover the cost of education. Similarly, in the rural southeastern United States, several colleges have traditionally used school enterprises to help support themselves (Mullinax and others, 1991). One of these, Berea College, has had students working in more than sixty different departments, including a bakery, wood shop, farm, dairy, restaurant, and hotel, in addition to the college's power plant, maintenance and housekeeping, library, and administrative offices (Peck, 1989).

The possibility for profitable school enterprise also exists in more affluent settings. (Chapters Two and Four contain information about the revenues produced by the SBEs we studied.) However, in relatively prosperous places such as the United States, the potential monetary revenues from SBEs are of less interest than the possible educational benefits. According to von Borstel, the eighteenth-century French philosopher Jean Jacques Rousseau was the first to assert the pedagogical benefits of productive education. Rousseau's ideas were applied and refined by the Swiss-German educator Johann Heinrich Pestalozzi, who opened a school in 1774 in which education was organized around productive labor. Among other nineteenth-century proponents of the pedagogical value of work were the French uto-

pian socialist Charles Fourier and the German schoolmaster Georg
Kershensteiner. The American philosopher John Dewey brought
this idea into the twentieth century, consistently arguing that
students learn best when productive experience is an integral
part of their education. Some of these older arguments have been
given new support by recent cognitive science (Berryman, 1992).

In industrialized countries, the use of school-based enterprise for educational purposes has been relatively more frequent in connection with professional and vocational schooling.
Teaching hospitals attached to medical schools are a well-known
example. Similarly, many law schools publish law review journals that are written and produced mainly or entirely by students (Fidler, 1983; Riggs, 1981). Attorneys and judges rely
on law reviews for in-depth analysis of legal issues and identification of trends. And at the highest levels of formal schooling,
doctoral students in the physical, biological, and social sciences
routinely work in research projects, the product of which is new
knowledge, and all doctoral students are required to produce
a piece of original research in order to obtain their degrees. For
similar reasons, vocational and technical programs in high
schools and two-year colleges organize SBEs to give students
practice producing useful goods or services. In particular, marketing education programs have included instruction in entrepreneurship, guiding students through the process of researching
the market, writing a business plan, obtaining a loan, producing and selling a product or service, and liquidating the enter
prise (Stone, 1989). At all levels, these SBEs provide a means
for students to learn their craft.

School-based enterprise has less frequently been applied
to students in the "academic" tracks of high school and college.
Despite the protests of Dewey and others, high school curricula
that prepare students for further education have been divorced
from programs that prepare students for work. The academic
curriculum has generally eschewed practical applications at the
high school and college level, although students at the highest
levels of postgraduate education routinely participate in various
forms of school-based enterprise. However, some SBEs have
sprung from high school academic courses. Perhaps the best-

known example in the United States is Foxfire, a literary enterprise that started in an English class and has published a series of magazines and books (Wigginton, 1986). Other examples are found in courses dealing with environmental science, where students collect and publish data on the quality of local water, soil, and air (OECD, 1991).

The usefulness of school-based enterprise to teach academic subject matter in elementary and secondary schools has been well illustrated in Great Britain, where the government in 1986 began to promote "mini-enterprises" (Jamieson, Miller, and Watts, 1988). These were patterned originally on the model developed since 1963 by a not-for-profit extracurricular organization called Young Enterprise, itself modeled on the Junior Achievement program that was started in the United States in 1919 by the Chamber of Commerce for the purpose of teaching the principles of capitalist enterprise. Junior Achievement is still active in this country, mainly as an extracurricular activity. In Great Britain, on the other hand, mini-enterprises are part of the school curriculum. They are explicitly designed to develop students' understanding of concepts and information from academic subjects, including mathematics, English, social studies, physical science, technology, and computers (Williams, 1991).

In the 1990 Carl Perkins Vocational and Applied Technology Education Act Amendments, the U.S. Congress changed the law that authorizes federal support for vocational education. Instead of keeping vocational and academic curricula separate, the 1990 law requires federal money for vocational education to be spent only on programs that integrate the academic and vocational. This law, and the developments in cognitive science that provided part of the rationale for it, may stimulate the creation of more SBEs and other practical applications that encompass academic as well as vocational objectives. Chapter Three explains how the SBEs we studied approach a range of learning objectives.

In addition to covering some of the costs of schooling and helping students learn, SBEs have also been created to provide benefits to people outside the school. One example is the use of schools as seedbeds for new enterprises that add to the economic base of the community or region by exporting goods or services. These enterprises are generally either turned over to local businesses or continued by students after they leave school. Jonathan Sher (1977) proposed the concept of school-based community development corporations that would perform this function in rural communities. Subsequently, Sher and Paul DeLargy created an organization called REAL (Rural Entrepreneurship Through Action Learning), which has enabled rural schools in fifteen states to spawn new businesses that add to the local export base (*The REAL Story,* Fall/Winter 1992).

SBEs have also been created to provide benefits to local communities in the form of information or other services. For example, Mullenax (1982) has described a school in rural Colombia called the FUNDAEC Rural University, which offered a six-year program to train "engineers for rural development." As part of the program, the school developed and demonstrated more productive methods for agriculture in the region. Students helped local farmers implement the new techniques. The school thus took on the function of an agricultural extension service, dispensing free information. Similarly, in the urban United States, schools have engaged students in giving information to local communities about issues including health and nutrition, energy conservation, and disaster preparedness. Some of these activities are included in what has been called "service learning": community service to teach citizenship.

The promotion of prosocial values has provided the impetus for school-based enterprise at various times and in various places. Combining education with production has been advocated as a method to teach appreciation for all labor and to avoid developing elitist attitudes among students who are privileged to receive more than the average amount of schooling (van Rensburg, 1974). This has been an explicit objective for school-based enterprise in socialist countries, but it has also been emphasized by nonsocialists (including Kershensteiner and Dewey). On the other hand, Junior Achievement and, initially, the British mini-enterprise initiative have used school-based enterprise to teach appreciation for market capitalism. Contemporary American

SBEs are concerned with fostering students' sense of responsibility for the quality of the goods or services they produce. Chapters Five through Seven offer examples of how SBEs confront students with this and other questions of value.

School-Based Enterprises Versus Nonschool Jobs

There has not yet been any systematic evaluation of SBEs to test whether they have achieved their educational and social purposes. Such an evaluation would require control groups and, preferably, random assignment of students to the program and control groups. Data on both groups would have to be collected for a number of years during and after the program. Unfortunately, we do not have any such data to offer here.

We do have some testimonial evidence from a small group of students who were participating in SBEs and also holding paid jobs outside of school at the same time. We found these students among a larger sample we were surveying to find out about the effects of working while in school. The sample includes high school students from five locations in different regions of the United States. Baseline surveys were administered in the fall of 1988 in two districts and the fall of 1989 in three other districts. In each school, some students were employed at the time of the survey and others were not. Further description of the sample and questionnaires can be found in Stern, Stone, Hopkins, and McMillion (1990).

Table 1.1 contains baseline data from juniors and seniors in four districts, two in the Midwest and two in the Southeast. These particular students were participating in SBEs in addition to holding paid jobs outside of school. (Students whose paid jobs were supervised by the school under a cooperative education program are not included here.) Students were asked a set of questions about their out-of-school jobs and a parallel set of questions about their work in SBEs. Table 1.1 shows responses to all questions for which there was a statistically significant difference between the students' characterization of their experience in SBEs and in outside jobs.

The differences in Table 1.1 reveal, first of all, that students think SBEs are more closely related than nonschool jobs to their education. Several questions about use of math on the job, one question about reading, and one question about writing all indicate that SBEs give students more opportunity to apply on the job what they are learning in school. Direct questions about whether the job lets them practice what they learned in school give the same result. Evidently, these students find that their SBE experience reinforces school learning more strongly than their outside jobs do.

SBEs also give students more opportunity to learn new things, as indicated by three questions that ask this directly. Two other questions indicate that SBEs more often confront students with the necessity to think: when they are unclear about what they have to do on the job and when they feel that they have too much work to do everything well. The only thing that students learn more about in outside jobs is how to manage money — not surprising, since most work in SBEs is unpaid.

One limitation of SBEs is that most of the people involved are students; thus SBEs contribute less than outside jobs to broadening students' range of social contacts, especially with people over age thirty. The absence of pay also has an effect on socializing: SBEs do not enable students to go out as often as nonschool jobs do. On the other hand, unlike work in outside jobs, work in SBEs does not cause students to see their friends less often.

Some Hard Questions

These results, which are consistent with those found by Stern (1984), indicate that engaging in production combined with schooling may have greater educational value for students than participating in school and work as unrelated activities. Indeed, it would be surprising if productive activity organized by the school did not have more educational content than outside jobs. What remains to be shown, however, is that SBEs have greater educational merit than ordinary classroom activities. Granted that school-based enterprise can improve work, can it also improve school?

We do not propose to settle that question in this book.

Table 1.1. Significant Differences Between Students' Experiences in
SBEs and in Non-School-Supervised Jobs Off Campus.[a]

	Percent of Respondents Answering Yes	
	SBE	Nonschool Job
Use of Knowledge and Skill Acquired in School		
Do you read safety rules and instructions in the use and maintenance of equipment and tools? (n = 20)	70.0	35.0
Do you read job manuals? (n = 20)	65.0	20.0
Do you use addition, subtraction, multiplication, and division; make change; perform simple measurements? (n = 21)	90.5	42.9
Do you compute or figure ratios, fractions, percents, and decimals; draw and interpret graphs? (n = 21)	47.6	4.8
Do you compute or figure discounts, markups, selling prices? (n = 21)	47.6	14.3
Do you calculate surface area, volume, or weights; calculate plane and solid figures; solve simple equations (use algebra)? (n = 21)	38.1	4.8
Do you apply fractions, percentages, proportions, ratios, algebra, geometry to solve work problems? (n = 21)	47.6	9.5
Do you print or write simple sentences? (n = 19)	63.2	36.8

	Percent of Respondents	
	SBE	Nonschool Job
My job gives me a chance to practice what I learned in school. (n = 26)		
Not at all true	3.8	42.3
A little true	23.1	42.3
Somewhat true	30.8	7.7
Very true	42.3	7.7
To what extent does your job make use of special skills you learned in school? (n = 26)		
Not at all	11.5	38.5
A little	11.5	30.8
Some	42.3	11.5
A great deal	34.6	19.2

Table 1.1. Significant Differences Between Students' Experiences in SBEs and in Non-School-Supervised Jobs Off Campus[a], Cont'd.

	SBE	Nonschool Job
This job uses my skills and abilities.[b] (n = 26)		
Not at all true	3.8	11.5
A little true	19.2	30.8
Somewhat true	34.6	26.9
Very true	42.3	30.8
Opportunity to Learn New Things		
This job gives me a chance to learn a lot of new things. (n = 26)		
Not at all true	3.8	15.4
A little true	15.4	30.8
Somewhat true	26.9	38.5
Very true	53.8	15.4
Sometimes I am unclear about what I have to do on this job. (n = 25)		
Not at all true	20.0	60.0
A little true	40.0	12.0
Somewhat true	32.0	24.0
Very true	8.0	4.0
How much has this job helped you learn to manage your money? (n = 26)		
Not at all	42.3	11.5
A little	11.5	19.2
Some	26.9	46.2
A great deal	19.2	23.1
I have too much work to do everything well. (n = 26)		
Not at all true	30.8	57.7
A little true	30.8	30.8
Somewhat true	23.1	11.5
Very true	15.4	0.0
To what extent does your job teach you new skills that will be useful in your future work?[b] (n = 26)		
Not at all	7.7	19.2
A little	11.5	26.9
Some	46.2	26.9
A great deal	34.6	26.9

Table 1.1. Significant Differences Between Students' Experiences in
SBEs and in Non-School-Supervised Jobs Off Campus[a], Cont'd.

	SBE	Nonschool Job
Do you think that the things you are learning in this job will be useful to you in your later life?[b] (n = 25)		
Extremely useful	32.0	12.0
Very useful	20.0	16.0
Somewhat useful	40.0	48.0
Not at all useful	8.0	24.0
Opportunity for Social Contacts		
How much has this job helped you learn to communicate with others? (n = 26)		
Not at all	8.0	0.0
A little	16.0	4.0
Some	28.0	32.0
A great deal	48.0	64.0
To what extent does your job let you get to know people over age thirty? (n = 26)		
Not at all	34.6	3.8
A little	19.2	23.1
Some	26.9	30.8
A great deal	19.2	42.3
Because of this job, I see my friends less often than I used to. (n = 24)		
Not at all true	62.5	25.0
A little true	16.7	33.3
Somewhat true	12.5	20.8
Very true	8.3	20.8
Because I have more money, I am able to go out with my friends more often. (n = 25)		
Not at all true	64.0	24.0
A little true	8.0	32.0
Somewhat true	28.0	32.0
Very true	0.0	12.0
How much time do you spend with other workers who are about your age on your job? (n = 25)		
All the time	68.0	28.0
More than half the time	12.0	0.0
Half the time	4.0	20.0

Table 1.1. Significant Differences Between Students' Experiences in
SBEs and in Non-School-Supervised Jobs Off Campus[a], Cont'd.

	SBE	Nonschool Job
Less than half the time	4.0	20.0
Only a little time	0.0	16.0
No time at all	12.0	16.0

[a]Except where noted, all differences are statistically significant at $p < 0.05$.
For questions with yes or no answers, significance determined by binomial test.
For other questions, significance determined by Wilcoxon test.

[b]Statistically significant at $p < 0.10$.

Our intent here is simply to get more people thinking about
it. Chapters Three through Five offer evidence of a preliminary
kind. It is anecdotal; it is testimonial. But the repetition of anec-
dotes and testimony in the SBEs we have studied is striking.
Something of educational value seems to be happening here.

The next question is, If school-based enterprise offers significant educational benefits, why is it not already a central part
of most students' high school experience? This is what Chapters Six and Seven are about. They describe the difficulties and
dilemmas of starting and running an SBE.

In Chapter Eight, we turn to the question, How can these
difficulties be overcome so that more students can obtain the
benefits of school-based enterprise? We imagine two examples
of schools that use school-based enterprise as the organizing force
for an entire curriculum. In Chapter Nine, we also offer proposals for supporting existing SBEs and stimulating formation
of new ones.

2

Enterprise in Action: Examples from Sixteen Schools

*T*he following five chapters discuss the benefits and problems of SBEs. Those chapters blend observations from sixteen case studies. In this chapter, we show a snapshot of each case by itself, to help readers identify the sites as we discuss them later and to illustrate the range of situations in which SBEs occur.

Selection of Case Study Sites

Searching for SBEs to study, we began by sending a letter of inquiry to state commissioners or superintendents of education and state vocational directors in all fifty states, the District of Columbia, and U.S. territories. The letter requested nominations for exemplary or innovative SBE programs.

Nominations were received from thirty-four states, Guam, and Puerto Rico. Nine of the states submitted only one nomination; five submitted more than ten. Additions to the sample frame were generated from published sources. This dual process yielded 165 nominations — secondary and postsecondary — that created the initial sampling frame. These included thirteen manufacturing enterprises, twenty-two house-building or construction projects, thirty-one food-service operations, thirty-four

16

retail enterprises, thirty-five that were classified as personal services (including cosmetology, child care, banking, and auto
repair), nineteen agricultural enterprises, and eleven miscel-
laneous.

Forty-three sites were selected for initial screening. We
were seeking a variety of enterprises: projects that were part
of traditional vocational programs, some where the focus was
on academic development, others that integrated academic and
vocational education, and projects where the focus was on community development or where the enterprise was a seedbed for
individual entrepreneurship. We contacted these forty-three sites
by telephone in the spring of 1991. During these telephone interviews, we sought to determine the number of students and
teachers involved, duration and intensity of the SBE, learning
objectives, customer base, annual revenues (if any), whether
the model had been copied elsewhere, and whether there was
an emphasis on teaching all aspects of the industry.

As a result of those interviews, the sixteen sites described
below were selected for inclusion in this study. At several sites
(Fairfax County, Hocking College, Metro Tech, and Warren
Tech), more than one SBE was examined. During 1991 and
1992, two or more of the authors visited each site (except Marion
County, which received only one visitor). During each site visit,
we followed a protocol that outlined interviews with the school
administrator, the teacher(s), and other adults involved with
the enterprise. A group interview of students involved with the
enterprise was also conducted. We observed the enterprise in
operation on one or more occasions during the visit. These interviews and observations were supplemented by written materials provided by each school.

SBEs in Comprehensive High Schools

Comprehensive high schools prepare students for both college
and work, usually in separate programs. Most SBEs are part
of a work-related curriculum, but some also occur on the college-
preparatory, academic side.

Fairfax County

Fairfax County is a large, wealthy suburb of Washington, D.C. Its school system has more than 130,000 students and twenty-three high schools. In 1972 the county established a foundation to promote interaction between the school system, students, administrators, teachers, local governments, the private sector, and the public at large.

Under the aegis of this Foundation for Applied Technical/ Vocational Education, Inc., Fairfax County sponsors a county-wide SBE program of major proportions. Much of the initial funding and ongoing support for the various SBEs comes from this foundation, which often provides the seed money for projects and has, for example, financed a house-building operation.

We studied three programs in which the foundation played a part: the Classroom on the Mall, an automotive dealership, and a housing construction project. There are plans to add other programs as well. One teacher, for example, would like to turn a travel marketing program into a travel agency to enable students to learn more of the business than just making reservations. There is also a tentative plan to open a service facility at Dulles International Airport to teach aircraft mechanics.

The Classroom on the Mall program operates in three different shopping malls. In the branch that we studied, it provides entrepreneurial experiences through the operation of a seasonal gift shop known as the Marketplace. Approximately fifty-five students, mainly juniors and seniors, are given responsibility for planning, managing, and operating the store. The entire SBE is considered a marketing class. Businesspeople in the mall are involved with the program as speakers, part-time employers, and advisory committee members. The concept originated with the manager of the mall, who is a member of the school's marketing education advisory committee. Classroom space is also donated by the mall.

The store operates during two six-week selling periods. These are aligned with the mall's two busiest seasons, one from mid-November to Christmas Eve and the other around Easter.

The store is housed in a kiosk that is assembled for a selling season.

Two sets of students operate the store in shifts. From 10 A.M. to 1:30 P.M., the store is staffed by students earning course credit in the marketing class. Between 1:30 P.M. and closing at 9:30 P.M., the students are paid minimum wage. Managers earn an additional $.50 an hour. Half of the paid students use this as their cooperative education placement for the marketing class. The other half are nonmarketing students who work in the store simply as a part-time job. The total payroll is about $6,000 to $7,000 each year.

The inventory carried in the store is valued, on average, at $3,000, with another $2,000 in backup inventory stored in the classroom. By contrast, small commercial stores in the mall carry about $15,000 of inventory. The store's daily revenue ranges from $20 to $300. Students are responsible for buying merchandise from a local wholesaler. They are authorized to spend $4,000 to $5,000 for the spring season and $5,000 to $6,000 for the Christmas season. The Foundation for Applied Technical/Vocational Education receives all revenues and pays all expenses, including payroll.

Two teachers with extensive experience in retailing oversee the Marketplace. Four student store managers are selected by the teachers from volunteers. They undergo two days of specific training that includes everything from payroll issues to prevention of shoplifting. The student managers initially teach store procedures to other students and then move into a troubleshooting role. Students themselves are responsible for interviewing and rating applicants for jobs in the store, but teachers do the actual hiring, based in part on these ratings as well as a rating by the applicant's other teachers. Grades are not a factor in selection.

The Classroom on the Mall program began in 1978 and has had the consistent support of local businesses. As it has grown and evolved, it has involved students in both the operation and planning. A significant change occurred in 1991–92, when the teachers instituted a new organizational structure, grouping students into teams responsible for seasonal soft goods, seasonal hard goods, nonseasonal soft goods, and nonseasonal hard goods. (This experiment is described further in Chapter Three.) Students' involvement in planning and analyzing the Marketplace program occurs in part through term papers, which are required each quarter. In their papers, students might, for example, reevaluate the Marketplace's pricing policy during an economic recession or analyze the market segment they are serving.

The second SBE that we studied in Fairfax County is the house-building program. In a northern Virginia suburb of Washington, D.C., a neat subdivision of ten Georgian brick two-story houses can be seen among the trees. Only some fancy touches in the brickwork of the chimneys and corners would give a clue that these houses were not ordinary commercial products but were built by students.

The housing construction program started almost casually in 1971, when the county wanted to build some low-cost residences for groups of students visiting Washington, D.C. The original bid was too high, and it was discovered that students could do the work for one-third the cost. The first house was built on county-owned land, resulting in further cost reduction. However, surrounding landowners resisted the project, fearing it would not meet neighborhood standards of quality and aesthetics. There were also objections to using county taxes to subsidize housing. The foundation stepped in and provided both project financing and quality assurance. This began an annual series of home-building projects. By the eighth house, profits were sufficient to finance the next house without a bank loan. The tenth house sold for $525,000 in 1991, enabling the foundation to develop an adjacent tract of land on which students are scheduled to build an additional six homes.

Initial concern about competing with local builders has also dissipated: when builders started visiting the site, they were impressed by the excellent work being done by the students. They now support the program, and they have reportedly hired a number of its graduates.

The program has a detailed set of competencies that a student should acquire after two years (1,080 hours). With those competencies, students are considered qualified as construction helpers. Program staff stress that classroom training should not end at graduation, however; blueprint reading and estimating courses are considered necessary for eventual qualification as journey workers or independent contractors.

The program teaches conventional "stick" construction: all framing is cut on site. However, the industry trend is toward panelization, in which large pieces of the house are built at the factory and shipped to the site intact. As technological evolution continues, it will require a change in training methods.

The third foundation-supported SBE we studied is Student Auto Sales, a used-car dealership. It was initiated by the foundation in 1984 to provide competent workers for the automotive service industry. Operated by students under teachers' supervision, the dealership meets all state licensing and insurance requirements. It has the support of local auto dealers, who find that the benefits of a supply of trained workers outweigh the slight loss of business that the dealership represents. The dealers offer both operating advice and technical advice on particularly difficult problems.

The program consists of three parts: mechanical repair, body repair, and operations and sales. Cars are acquired by the teachers for repair and refurbishment and then are sold through the sales program. Most cars are donated and are about four to five years old. Before any work is done, a cost analysis is completed by students and compared with the market value of the car as determined by local research. A car is then sent to be repaired prior to sale, kept for parts, or used as an instructional device. A car that is to be sold must pass a state safety inspection.

Students usually participate in the program for two years, but a training sequence as long as four years is available. The emphasis is on entry-level skills. Students are organized into teams, each led by an experienced student. Each car is the responsibility of one team.

A typical scenario at the dealership would have seven cars for sale, with a total inventory value of $9,000. The dealership is open during regular business hours each day and has two special sales each year. Total revenue was about $68,000 in fiscal 1991, yielding $16,000 in gross profit. All of this profit goes to the foundation, which uses it to purchase special equipment and to support student scholarships.

Students also repair cars owned by customers. No labor costs are charged, but customers pay for parts and pay a small shop fee. This work yields about $12,000 a year in revenue, which is placed in a school account and used to pay for parts and shop supplies.

About fifty students perform mechanical work supervised by a degreed teacher with industry experience. About thirty-five students repair auto bodies under supervision of a licensed teacher with twenty-five years of direct experience. Almost all students are male.

New students spend nine weeks in the classroom before they are assigned to a team and allowed into the dealership. After that they continue to receive formal training in the form of lectures and workbook assignments. The teachers are careful to acquire cars that represent a wide range of learning situations. However, there is little integration with other school subjects.

Southington High School

The high school in Southington, a small city in Connecticut, draws its students from comfortable neighborhoods. In many ways, it is a prototypical American high school, but it has had a long involvement with school-based enterprise and also with mentally handicapped students.

The school store opened in 1968. It is run by students as one of four components of the marketing education program. The other three components are classroom instruction, cooperative education, and membership in DECA (Distributive Education Clubs of America). DECA membership is vigorously encouraged, and DECA competitions are both entered and won.

Six students at a time staff the store. Two students work the cash register terminals. The lead student actually handles a transaction, while the second student, usually a trainee, gets the merchandise. This informal student-to-student training is supported by a training manual. The on-the-job experience, which is coordinated with the marketing education program curriculum, involves students in a range of interactions with customers. The students work in a rotation that takes them out of their formal class about one hour every nine days.

The instructors handle most of the money after the students balance out at the end of each class period. Annual revenue is about $50,000, yielding $12,000 to $15,000 profit, which is used to support the local DECA chapter's activities, conferences, and field trips. The store is audited every summer.

A doughnut concession yields another $2,000 to $3,000 a year. This money goes into a student activity fund. A fax machine for school use was purchased from this fund in 1991, for example, and some of the doughnut money is used by the principal to help students with outside activities such as an awards banquet for academic winners, band events, and defraying the cost of attending student conferences.

Three teachers take turns monitoring the store when it is open. They also balance the books. New emphasis is being placed on cooperation between vocational and academic disciplines, and one of the teachers is on a committee to initiate interdisciplinary projects. For example, marketing and business education are working with the math department to create a curriculum unit on market research.

Southington is continuing to develop new SBEs. In 1992 it opened a small supermarket on campus to train developmentally and learning disabled students. Equipment, uniforms, and initial inventory were donated by the ShopRite chain, which has contributed to similar programs in five other states. Other local markets have also provided support. Only teachers from the high school are eligible to shop there initially. Proceeds from sales will be used to replenish the inventory. A competency-based curriculum appropriate to special-needs students, developed at Cornell University, is used in the program.

Marketing education students are also extending the program by setting up stores in a local hospital and a nursing home. There are plans to establish a bank (and possibly a credit union) that will be owned and operated by students.

Rindge School of Technical Arts

The Rindge School of Technical Arts, which describes itself as the second-oldest vocational school in the country, is now one of six schools that comprise Cambridge Rindge and Latin School, serving Cambridge, Massachusetts. The other five are academic schools: a fundamental school with a strict dress code, an academic preparatory school, and three different versions of comprehensive schools. The six schools educate a highly diverse group of 2,100 students. Cambridge is primarily a working-class city with a study body from sixty-four countries, but the school is also striving to serve the children of Harvard professors and other affluent residents of this Boston suburb. The Rindge technical/vocational program has been relatively unpopular. Although it offers a range of vocational programs, including computer graphic arts and robotics, its total enrollment is only slightly over 200 students, with perhaps another 300 students coming from the other five schools to take occasional courses. However, Rindge has a new principal, Larry Rosenstock, whose prior employment includes teaching carpentry and being staff attorney with the Center for Law and Education, which is based in Cambridge, Massachusetts, and Washington, D.C. The school is planning major curriculum changes.

We studied the culinary arts program, which graduated nine seniors in 1991. All the graduates are either employed or taking advanced study in culinary arts. The director, Joel Legault, is a former restaurant chef in his thirties who became interested in teaching through working with Little League baseball players. The second teacher, Ingrid Motsis, from Denmark, directs the baking program. The two are assisted by Brenda Binder, who grew up in North Dakota. The program enrolls mainly at-risk students.

The school restaurant prepares lunch each day for fifty to seventy teachers and school staff members. It operates primarily as a cafeteria, with the student cooks working in full view of the clientele behind steam tables and over the grill and a student at the cash register, but it is also called upon to provide sit-down lunches or coffee for the many visitors that Rindge receives. The emphasis is on training students to work as cooks rather than preparing them for the day when they might run their own restaurant. The realism of preparing food for real customers and the pressure of having to meet a daily time schedule are important parts of the learning process. In the recent past, the culinary school ran a sit-down restaurant that was open for lunch to the community. The restaurant received a favorable newspaper review from Julia Child, who lives nearby. Despite this success, however, the change was made to a cafeteria format so that students would spend more of their time preparing food and less time waiting tables and busing.

Rothsay High School

The 1986 closing of the only lumberyard in rural Rothsay, Minnesota, created a vacuum that resulted in an ambitious SBE. It also changed the community's relationship with the high school. The community itself has become the school, and the small size of the town is seen as a major virtue that necessitates creativity and innovation.

High school students reopened the lumberyard and hardware store, saving Rothsay residents from having to drive forty miles round-trip to another town for a hinge or a last-minute gift. The hardware store and lumberyard are run as one business. They stock a range of goods and carry an inventory worth about $50,000. Lumber provides 10 percent of sales, hardware 60 percent, housewares 15 percent, and paint 15 percent.

The revival of the business as a school enterprise began when the school district bought the building for $20,000. The district then received a $30,000 grant for inventory from the West Central Minnesota Initiative Fund. This grant will have to be repaid if the business does not remain in operation at least five years. The local Rothsay Community Development corporation contributed another $30,000 to get the project started.

The hardware store does not compete on price against stores in larger cities nearby. (It is considered improper for SBEs to compete with taxpayers using tax money.) Instead, retail customers pay a little more for the convenience of having a store in town. The SBE's main supplier sells at a 21 percent markup over cost — 15 percent plus a 6 percent shipping charge — which determines pricing in the hardware store. Local contractors expect a discount on lumber, however.

Two former store employees have returned from retirement to help the program, because neither the teachers nor the principal had had exactly this type of retail experience. However, the teachers have worked hard and inspired enthusiasm in the students, some of whom have come to the store of their own volition to shovel snow as needed and have volunteered to clean out the yard in response to a caution from the fire marshal.

The store has fourteen different types of jobs, each with a job description. Male and female students help customers, operate cash registers, and write quarterly reports to the SBE's sponsors. Little marketing is done, and advertising is somewhat casual. Many students are not aiming for business careers, but they value the experience the store provides and know they are doing something useful for the community.

Encouraged by their success in operating the hardware store and lumberyard, school officials helped a group of teenagers form their own corporation in 1991. Owned and managed by students, the company is named Tiger, Inc., after the school mascot and as an acronym for Teenage Innovative Group, Entrepreneurs of Rothsay. Two months after the corporation was established, the community's only grocery store failed. Tiger, Inc., took it over and soon reopened it. In 1992–93 the business was grossing more than $300,000 a year. The annual payroll of $40,000 goes mainly to teenagers. The high school offers mentorship classes at the grocery store in meat cutting, accounting, and store management. Tiger, Inc., is also acting as a small-business incubator on the model of a REAL enterprise. It has helped two students open a fitness center and tanning salon called the Body Shop, for example. Another group of students wrote a business plan to market Native American craftwares in Scandinavia, and this activity was getting under way in 1993.

Belle Fourche High School

Belle Fourche, a four-year high school, enrolls about 350 students from a sparsely settled area of South Dakota ranches and farms. The concept of entrepreneurship permeates the entire curriculum. Groups of students run SBEs linked to both academic and vocational courses. Entrepreneurship by individuals and groups of students is also encouraged.

SBEs flourish in connection with vocational subjects, including masonry, plumbing, cabinetry, carpentry, occupational foods, and agriculture. In addition, a writing program begun in 1982 now features individual writers from the creative writing class and produces children's books in a children's literature course. Belle Fourche also has two special education programs.

A number of enterprises have been started by students and are now sustaining themselves outside of the school system. Sheldon Enterprises, for example, makes and markets coin banks. Cockleburr Country developed and copyrighted a caricature that is used on its various gifts, such as sweatshirts, cards, and pencils. Other SBE spin-offs include printing, computer programming, and auto-detailing businesses.

Not all SBEs have remained successful, however. For example, in the late 1980s, one class built and decorated a snack shop called THIS, Inc., which became commercially successful. As time passed, the founders' departure caused momentum to be lost and the purpose forgotten. Minor thefts bedeviled the project, and it was eventually closed. From this experience, teachers learned the importance of maintaining students' commitment and of planning how a project will end.

Various philosophical concerns have also arisen—issues such as how much vocational instruction a comprehensive high school should give before a program is passed on to a vocational school and the benefits of economic rewards versus the wisdom of giving away labor. In addition, the underlying idea that all students are entrepreneurs was resisted by some of the faculty, and there are still questions about how SBEs are linked to students' future plans. And each program has its own individual concerns. Competition with local businesses has been a major issue in Belle Fourche's construction programs, for example.

The prevailing attitude at Belle Fourche views the school as the whole community, not something confined within classroom walls. That attitude gives students and teachers unusual freedom. The teaching staff can decide when, what, and who will teach, and they choose the textbooks. Educational activity, which has broadened from teaching skills to creating employment, is now becoming a way of life. A new emphasis on rural economic development is giving the school the potential to become an even more important force in the community.

Brooks County High School

Brooks County High School, in rural Georgia, operates a child-care center for students and the community. Located in a town of 5,000 people, Brooks is the only public high school in the county. Enrollment is about 850 students, of whom about two-thirds are African American and many are poor. Brooks County is the leading recipient of food stamps in Georgia.

The child-care center began in 1980 as part of the first project sponsored by REAL enterprises. However, it does not represent the kind of project REAL has sponsored more recently.

The state-licensed child-care program serves the community at large, students who are parents, and a foster-care service. It enrolls more than fifty children, from newborns to those of kindergarten age. A flat daily fee is charged, based on income, regardless of the time each child spends there. The fee is close to what is charged by the other day-care center in town so as to avoid price competition. Revenue from fees is sufficient to pay for four aides, a director, and supplies. The program is housed in its own facility, which includes a kitchen and toilets.

Since fees are based on income, they must be kept confidential. This means that students have no contact with the financial aspects of the center. They do study all other aspects, however, as part of a two-year program. Unlike most SBEs, this one is actively monitored by state authorities, including the health, fire, and human resource departments. Thus students are exposed to the realities of running a child-care center. Informal followup studies have found a number of graduates in day-care jobs and others establishing day-care services in their homes. Other former students work with the elderly.

The center has been found effective in preparing young children for school. An evaluation showed that school readiness is greater for children who spend their kindergarten year at the SBE than for children who attend private kindergartens.

Like other SBEs, this program continues to evolve. A parenting program is being started for twenty-four student parents to help parents in high school finish and to recover some who have dropped out. The SBE will offer free child care as part of that program.

Mt. Edgecumbe High School

Unique among the SBEs we studied, the enterprise at Mt. Edgecumbe High School (MEHS) uses a systematic quality-improvement process that suffuses the whole curriculum. MEHS is a state-supported residential high school located on an island across from Sitka, on the coast of southeast Alaska. Timber and fish processing are locally important industries. In 1991–92 85 percent of the 216 students enrolled were Alaskan Native, and 88 percent came from rural areas.

The curriculum at MEHS is designed to prepare students to participate in the commerce and culture of the Pacific Rim. The twenty-four credits required for graduation include four credits each in English and social studies, three credits each in math and science, two each in computers and health/physical education, and one each in Pacific Rim studies and foreign languages, in addition to electives. A school-conducted survey of 133 graduates in the spring of 1990 found 38 percent attending postsecondary education, 35 percent employed full-time, 8 percent combining school and work, 5 percent working as homemakers, 3 percent serving in the military, and 11 percent unknown or unemployed. These outcomes are more favorable than those generally achieved by rural Alaskan students.

Continuous improvement, based on monitoring of observable outcomes, is emphasized at MEHS for instructors, students, and administrators alike. The computer lab, and computer teacher David Langford, play an important part in this. The lab is centrally located, well equipped with networked Macintoshes, and open during the evening (staffed by student monitors). Students learn to use the computer for projects in their various classes and to keep track of their own learning. Langford is articulate in espousing the philosophy of continuous quality improvement and giving students responsibility for their own learning. Students and faculty from MEHS have made presentations on Total Quality Management and similar topics at a number of conferences, both for other educators and for noneducational audiences. The way MEHS has mobilized itself for continuous improvement has made it an example of a school serving as a model workplace.

School enterprise activity at MEHS has involved students in product development, marketing, and continuous improvement of the production process. The first product was lox, made from smoked sockeye salmon. MEHS superintendent Larrae Rocheleau brought the recipe and the production know-how with him when he came to MEHS in 1984. In his previous position as administrator of a small school district near Ketchikan, he had engaged students in preparing a relatively nice-looking, high-quality lox and had discovered an unexpectedly large demand for it among both the local population and tourists.

When Rocheleau brought in the teacher who had worked on this activity in his previous district, this product became the focus of an interdisciplinary project that has involved MEHS students for five years. But Rocheleau insisted that none of the lox would be sold domestically. Instead, students would try to export it to Japan. As the superintendent explains, "I wanted to force them to see why they were learning Japanese, why they were learning Pacific Rim cultures, why we require geography as a class here — how you integrate all those things." Problems included using computers to set up spreadsheets, figuring out transportation from Tokyo's Narita International Airport to Tokyo proper, and understanding what kind of export and import laws applied.

Students became involved in the enterprise through their classes in entrepreneurship, business applications, Pacific Rim studies, Japanese language, computers, art, and math. Each year for three years, a group of students and faculty visited Japan, in part to explore how to sell lox there. Japanese visitors also gave critiques on the quality of the fish and its packaging. However, Edgecumbe Enterprises never found a regular commercial channel for its lox in Japan. Instead, according to Rocheleau, "What we ended up doing is going to Alaska Pulp Company, a business here in Sitka that's Japanese-owned. They send a freighter to Japan once a month, and if you put in less than twenty-three pounds, you aren't subject to the import laws. So they put it in their freezer. Ship it on board and take it over for us and don't charge us. In essence, what they're doing is buying our salmon, taking it over, and then they distribute it, which is fine with us. We're getting $18 a pound for it." At its peak, the salmon-processing enterprise led by teacher Marty Johnson was producing approximately 2,000 pounds of lox and kippered salmon each year.

Entrepreneurship, an elective class, spends the most time on this activity. Students spend about half their time in this class actually cutting, curing, and packaging fish. Students also analyze these routine production tasks, seeking to improve both the quality of the product and the quality of their own working conditions. Much like a self-managed work team in a progressive corporation, students engage in continual problem identifica tion and problem solving. Another elective class, business applications, works with Edgecumbe Enterprises as one of its clients, keeping financial records, filling out tax and legal forms, and playing the part of strategic manager.

In 1991–92 Edgecumbe Enterprises was in transition. The superintendent and faculty wanted students to have the experience of starting another new enterprise. They advertised in the newspaper for companies to work with MEHS on this and received two bids. They accepted an offer from a local fish-processing company that wanted help in developing a new smoked salmon product for possible sale in gift selections of Alaskan produce. The company provided raw salmon to the class, which tested recipes. Meanwhile, the superintendent gave the lox recipe to another local company — one that was starting to process specialty salmon. The superintendent's strategy is to give students the opportunity to learn what goes into starting a new enterprise and at the same time to provide real services to local businesses.

SBEs in Multivocational Secondary Schools

Given the natural affinity between school-based enterprise and vocational or professional education, it is not surprising that SBEs are commonly found in specialized vocational schools. Here are some examples.

The High School of Cooperative and Technical Education

The visitor climbs a shaky but safe steel fire escape to the fifth floor, where a group of high school students are raising a twenty-four-foot four-by-twelve ceiling joist. They are standing on plywood sheathing nailed to a similar set of joists that they hung a few weeks earlier. Beside them is an open shaft that will eventually be the stairwell, dropping fifty feet to the ground below. The building is really only two sheer brick walls sixty feet high; the space between the walls has been occupied only by the ashes and debris of the fires that have ravaged the building since it was abandoned over twenty years ago. The students have begun the reconstruction of the building by removing the debris and erecting the beams and subfloors that will divide it into ten apartments. The building is located in Spanish Harlem in the Upper East Side of Manhattan. Twenty feet from the front of the building is the elevated railroad track, which only a mile south will go underground, hiding itself under Park Avenue on its way to Grand Central Station.

Sixty students work in this building. They all attend a New York City high school and spend alternate weeks in the building on a cooperative education plan. The students are over 95 percent male and over 90 percent minority: African Americans, Puerto Ricans, and first- and second-generation immigrants, mostly from the Caribbean and a dozen countries on the Latin American mainland. At the building site, they are divided into teams of three. Each team, along with a similar team from the preceding week's crew, will completely build one apartment over a two-year period. They are supervised by the five teachers in the building—one on each floor, mostly for safety reasons—who teach plumbing, electricity, and carpentry. At this stage, the electricity and plumbing students are doubling as carpenter's helpers, and the electricity and plumbing teachers take their lead from the two carpentry instructors in supervision. Later the roles will switch, as carpenters help with plumbing and wiring. Students also do drywall masonry and flooring work. They do virtually all the work in the building (except the exterior work, where the risk of falling is too great). The faculty, all licensed vocational education teachers with a career in construction behind them, do not perform any of the work; they only teach and supervise.

This SBE is sponsored by the High School of Cooperative and Technical Education, known as Coop Tech, a regional vocational school that teaches not only building trades but also welding, computer programming, machining, and the repair of air-conditioners, appliances, computers, and other pieces of electrical-mechanical equipment. Some Coop Tech students attend the school on a half-day basis, spending the other half-day in a regular comprehensive high school. Some, like the students at the construction site, are coop students one week in an academic school and then spend one week on site. A few Coop Tech students are high school graduates learning a trade.

The building project is an example of the complex partnership arrangements that are increasingly common in urban education. In this case, the partnership is four-way: the school has a written contract with the owners, who have complete responsibility for the building, including obtaining building licenses and arranging inspections, purchasing materials, providing liability insurance covering the students, and performing or commissioning those tasks that the school cannot train the students to do or that are considered too unsafe for students. The homeowners obtained the property from the city, which had claimed it for unpaid back taxes years earlier. The New York City Homestead Agency arranged for the "homesteaders" to purchase the building for a dollar. The students are paid minimum wage on the site through a federal program that sponsors youth employment and training.

The school has at any one time a dozen or more construction projects under way, each with a slightly different partnership arrangement. In some cases, the students and faculty are sent to perform a maintenance or remodeling project in another public school. They have a permanent teaching facility aboard the USS *Intrepid,* a decommissioned Navy aircraft carrier serving as a city museum, where the Coop Tech students do maintenance. Students have also done remodeling work for not-for-profit organizations such as museums and legitimate theaters, and they have worked with small private developers interested in restoring abandoned buildings to create subsidized low-income housing.

The High School of Cooperative and Technical Education is only a decade old, yet its future seems secure, with a growing demand on the part of students and clients. Principal Robert Yurasits argues that the same model should be put in place in four new buildings, one in each New York borough. However, there are no plans at present to create additional cooperative technical schools.

Metro Technical Institute

Metro Technical Institute is a vocational high school serving students in Phoenix, Arizona, many of whom are bused in from various home high schools. As the single vocational training center for the Phoenix area, it offers forty-three programs, several of which include SBE projects. One-third of Metro Tech students attend that school exclusively; the rest share their time with a home high school. The school emphasizes dropout prevention and recovery. The student population ranges from returning dropouts to students from the community college.

Metro Tech has been creative in forming various types of partnerships with local businesses and not-for-profit organizations. These have resulted in training on campus for off-campus jobs (for example, training phone reservationists) and contracting with a company to provide training (for example, in cosmetology). And some of these partnerships have resulted in SBEs. For example, a local aerospace company contracted with students from the computer-aided drafting class to transfer manual drawings onto computer files. A commercial credit union operates on campus, employing students. Building trades students do volunteer work with Habitat for Humanity and the corrections system.

In addition, Metro Tech has established SBEs on its own. The culinary arts program operates a coffee shop that feeds from forty to fifty customers a day and a deluxe dining room that serves 15,000 banquet meals a year. The horticulture program grows plants in the school's large greenhouses and sells potted plants and floral designs in a shop located in the "mini-mall" on campus. Floral design students also supply ten to fifteen weddings a year and provide the culinary arts program with table decorations and herbs.

Metro Tech administrators are concerned about developing students' academic skills and puzzle over how to integrate vocational and academic education. The difficulty arises in part from the traditional philosophy, held by some of the staff, that vocational education means teaching specific work skills only. Development of new teaching strategies is under way.

Warren Occupational Technical Center

Warren Occupational Technical Center is a secondary vocational school that has an articulation agreement with several community colleges. It serves approximately 1,000 students, predominantly white, with a faculty of one part-time and forty-two full-time instructors. Most teachers have master's degrees, and all have substantial industry work experience.

Some students drive their own cars, while others are bused in from the home high school where they take their academic courses. Postsecondary students earn credit that is transferred to the community college. A Warren Tech survey revealed that students' primary motivations for enrolling were employment and "getting a certificate in their field." They felt that the courses, often not offered through their home high school, were "more relevant" at Warren Tech.

School-based enterprise is pervasive at Warren Tech. The first principal, who had worked as a carpenter, machinist, and bricklayer, established a goal that each program would generate sufficient revenue to cover all costs except teachers' salaries. Warren Tech now offers vocational programs in twenty fields, and most of these incorporate school-based enterprise.

Students are not paid directly for work in SBEs. After one period of troublesome accounting, Warren instituted a very careful and thorough set of rules for the distribution of revenue from each SBE. Half the profit is reinvested into the program to replace equipment and purchase materials. The other half is split between funding a student activity account and campus improvement. Programs sometimes do work for each other, and any resulting transfers of money are included in the accounting.

Students in revenue-producing programs receive a major gift when they graduate. For example, mechanics graduating from an automotive program get a set of tools, and welders receive a full set of leathers.

Marion County Technical Center

Students at Marion County Technical Center have contributed a number of development projects to their West Virginia county. The Technical Center has offered occupational programs since 1979 for students from all of Marion County, which includes Fairmont, the county seat, and Mannington, a skeleton of a 1920s boom town. Within twenty miles of the Technical Center are West Virginia University, enrolling close to 21,000 students, and the state college at Fairmont, with enrollment over 6,000.

Mechanization of coal mining and other factors contributed to high unemployment and loss of population for more than three decades in Marion County. Hopes for a better economy are pinned on tourism and the pending relocation of a federal government records center to the county.

The economic situation in Marion County created a need for a series of community development projects, as revealed in a study conducted by the Future Farmers of America (FFA) agricultural education student group. This study was part of a nationally sponsored program called Building Our American Communities (BOAC). The Marion County FFA has been the national winner of the BOAC contest and is a strong contender every year. Nearly all of the projects have focused on increasing tourism. For example, the FFA is credited with valuable help in preserving a 1912 round barn of the Pennsylvania style that includes living quarters. Students converted it into a museum that displays agricultural machinery and small coal-mining items. The living quarters now provide space for community activities — for example, a weekly quilting group.

Students at Marion County Technical Center have helped the East August Historical Society take over a three-story school building and create another museum, where old school desks, oil-drilling equipment, and period furniture and period costumes are displayed, among other items of historical interest. The FFA displays its considerable history in its own section. On the same grounds is a log house that was moved from the adjoining county, refurbished, and opened to visitors.

In previous years, FFA students have restored an old train caboose to its original condition, saved a historic building that was once the carriage house of the richest person in the county, built park facilities, and conducted a survey for the county Tourist and Convention Bureau.

The latest BOAC project is tied more closely to the curriculum than most of the others. Students in the aquaculture course are using a demonstration pond to show how to grow fish in home ponds, helping residents improve their economic situation. This kind of economic development has been the mainstay of vocational agriculture for seventy-five years, but few have thought to make it a student led project for the BOAC competition.

SBEs for Selected Student Populations

In addition to serving the general cross sections of students found in comprehensive high schools and vocational secondary schools, SBEs have also been developed for selected groups of students. The following examples illustrate programs for the academically gifted, teenagers under court supervision, and young mothers.

Thomas Jefferson High School for Science and Technology

At Thomas Jefferson High School for Science and Technology (TJHSST), students produce and publish original scientific research. TJHSST was established in 1985 as the governor's school (one of a set of specialized schools) for science and technology in northern Virginia. About 400 students enroll in grades nine through twelve. A college-preparatory curriculum provides students with the opportunity for achievement in all disciplines, but the emphasis is on the sciences and technology. Admission is highly competitive, based on test scores, academic achievement, personal essays, and teacher recommendations. About 28 percent of the students represent minorities, and 57 percent of the students are male.

A distinguishing characteristic of TJHSST is a set of specialized technology laboratories — for example, life sciences and computer systems labs — that have been equipped by business and industry. All seniors are expected to complete a research project using these laboratories, although students may meet this requirement through off-campus research under the guidance of a mentor.

The mentoring program provides opportunities for students to do concentrated research under the leadership of an outside expert. Students selected for the program already exhibit a strong career interest and have demonstrated an equally strong academic preparation for the chosen field. Most mentorships run for one semester, but quite a few students decide to continue for a second semester. Some students in mentorships are paid, but most are not. The final output of the mentorship is a research paper, which is intended to be of publishable quality. Several of these papers have been published in engineering magazines and medical journals; many appear in TJHSST's own journal of students' original research.

In addition to producing new knowledge, mentorships enable students to do real work on real problems in settings outside the school, work with experts in their chosen field, work with adult professionals other than educators, and become employed, or employable, in the mentoring organization.

The Hollywood Diner

If SBEs require schools to behave in nontraditional ways, then a nontraditional school might best be able to accomplish the tasks involved in managing such an operation. The Hollywood Diner in Baltimore, run by such a school, provides an interesting site for observation. Created by the Chesapeake Center, a private school supported by contracts from the Department of Juvenile Services (DJS) of the State of Maryland, the Diner provides educational services to teenagers, age sixteen to twenty, who are under court supervision and who have had considerable difficulty in public school classrooms. Students are referred by the DJS. They must have better than sixth-grade math skills and be judged to be willing employees and stable students.

The goal is to help students develop the attitudes and skills of reliable employees and learn the restaurant trade, which offers many opportunities for employment. It is hoped that working in the Diner will help students gain confidence, self-respect, and maturity.

The Hollywood Diner began as the stage set in Barry Levinson's movie *Diner.* When the movie was completed, WBAL radio and others donated the building to the city, which converted it into a working restaurant with the idea of using it as a training site for unemployed youth. It was a financial failure. When the city offered to lease it for $1 a year, with the stipulation that the restaurant continue to train young workers, the Chesapeake Center, through its foundation, was its only bidder. In addition to sponsorship by the Center (which has achieved 100 percent job placement for its graduates, with zero recidivism), the Diner receives strong support from the mayor's office and the DJS.

Funding comes from diverse sources, funneled through the DJS, which is expected to fund training and administration costs. Having survived one false start, the Diner now appears on its way to fiscal stability, even though in its downtown location it faces considerable competition from other restaurants, bars, and delicatessens. This competition creates a realistic environment for the SBE.

Working in the Diner provides students with experience as servers, food preparers, cooks, and dishwashers. After hours, the trainees have opportunities to learn other jobs as they work in the Diner's catering business. The program also teaches job-readiness skills such as how to look for a job, interviewing techniques, expectations on the job, and so forth. Work-study projects are also assigned. At the time of our visit, at the end of 1991, the program had placed its first graduate with a large hotel chain and was training three more students, one as a cook, the other two as waiters.

The Diner supports two full-time adult employees. One is a cook with no social service training; the other is a counselor experienced with at-risk youth, who also has a background in restaurant management and catering.

The Diner offers breakfast and lunch on weekdays from 7:00 A.M. to 2:30 P.M. There is take-out service, as well as delivery within a limited area. On-site catering and after-hours private parties are related businesses that are actively pursued.

Located on an otherwise unusable piece of public land almost underneath an expressway in the central business district, the Hollywood Diner serves breakfast and lunch to office workers from nearby city agencies and private firms and construction workers in the area. Despite its barren surroundings, the Diner maintains a lively 1950s flair. Classic movie posters accent the gleaming, stainless-steel walls, and rock and roll blares from the chrome-plated jukebox. The Diner aims to be self-supporting, supplementing revenues from breakfast and lunch with money earned from private parties. The Diner's Hollywood image and decor add to the renaissance of downtown Baltimore, which has attracted national media attention over the past decade.

The program provides a new opportunity and a realistic learning environment for people who have been in trouble and need a mechanism to renew themselves. Thus it benefits both the community and the students. Community support has been encouraging. The future is clouded, however, because the Diner has failed as a restaurant in this location before. In addition, the project is dependent upon a great deal of volunteer support and funding, which can be transitory. Yet it remains an illustration of how a community can tackle its problems through imaginative ventures.

Laurence G. Paquin School

The Laurence G. Paquin School, also in Baltimore, is an alternative comprehensive high school at which expectant mothers can continue their education during pregnancy. After delivery, they can return to their home school, but some choose to remain at Paquin to take advantage of the many support services and the SBE learning opportunities.

The school gives its students the opportunity to continue and complete their education. It offers a special curriculum in family life, prenatal care, and parenting, along with a preschool center and an infant-toddler center. It also provides a variety of health, guidance-counseling, and social services. The school has about 300 students on the roll at any one time. Reflecting the population of Baltimore, students are predominantly African American, as are the principal and teaching staff. Each year the school serves over 1,000 students between the ages of eleven and twenty. With weekly entry and exit, many students do not attend Paquin full-time or for a full year.

Young Sensations is an enterprise in which Paquin students produce gift items and children's clothing and market their products both through a school-based boutique and, on consignment, in four area stores and two shopping malls. One product, a designer eyeglass case that students created, was sold wholesale at $10 and retailed in a boutique for $20. Young Sensations grossed $1,500 in fiscal 1990.

Many of the students have had no experience in sewing. Classroom instruction therefore begins with basic stitching, use of patterns, and selection and cutting of materials. Students continue learning until they are able to produce a variety of specialty items, including baby blankets, clothing for infants and toddlers, adolescent maternity wear, monogrammed sweatshirts and T-shirts, and gift and boutique items. Much of the teaching is done as one-to-one tutoring, since the students in any given class are at a wide range of technical skill development. Entrepreneurial skills are taught through self-study materials, lectures, and small-group projects.

Students in Young Sensations participate in decisions about what clothes to make and what designs to use, resulting in the production of a line of clothing especially tailored for the local market. They gain practical experience in merchandising, manufacturing, and small-business operations, including firsthand knowledge of the basic skills needed to become entrepreneurs. Work in Young Sensations is integrated with academic study through "writing across the curriculum." Students are required to complete written reports on a variety of topics. They are also encouraged to conduct personal interviews with entrepreneurs in connection with their writing.

The idea for the program came about when the school's principal, Rosetta Stith, observed a school in Jamaica where the students manufactured dolls that were sold through the school store. The director of the Young Sensations program, Wendy Parker-Robinson, is a graduate of Bennett College, Johns Hopkins University, and the Fashion Institute of Technology in New York City. At one time she operated her own boutique, making clothes of her own design. She received training from the Small Business Administration and now uses its entrepreneurial program as a foundation for her own instruction. Relationships with 4-H, the University of Maryland Cooperative Extension Office, and local businesses contribute to the curriculum and to ongoing staff development.

Though the school building is relatively modern, the SBE is jammed into a single large classroom with a small amount of adjoining storage space. The entire room is crowded, providing less space than the usual industrial setting and affording very little space for display of the products that Young Sensations manufactures. Thanks to a grant from a local foundation, one or two students can now be trained on a commercial-quality embroidery machine. The SBE also receives funding through the local home economics and business education program. School administrators and faculty hope that the program will eventually become self-sustaining through the sale of the students' products.

SBEs in Two-Year Colleges

Although the major focus of our attention in this book is high school, we also studied SBEs in two community colleges. These provide examples of what high schools might do.

Hocking Technical College

School-based enterprise is pervasive at Hocking Technical College, a two-year college located in Nelsonville, Ohio. The 5,000 students enrolled at Hocking make Nelsonville, with 5,000 inhabitants, a true college town. On a 250-acre campus situated in the Wayne National Forest, Hocking was started as a vocational school in 1968. Hocking faculty make vigorous use of their SBEs, which are strongly linked to the curriculum and provide a means for students to work their way through college. Only one-third of the college's funding comes from the state of Ohio.

Hocking's numerous SBEs contribute to learning and provide services not available in the community. The college owns the best hotel in town, a Quality Inn that serves as a training ground for students in the hospitality and food-service programs. Hocking is actively involved in the support of the community and hosts the annual Paul Bunyan Show, which attracts 55,000 tourists a year. In a more direct contribution to the private sector, the Ohio Technology Transfer Organization at the college provides marketing and technical assistance to local businesses. For example, a faculty member devised a telemarketing plan for a local shoe manufacturer and implemented the plan at Hocking's own telemarketing center, which is one of the SBEs.

Enterprises are both part of the curriculum and freestanding (to provide employment). An unusual feature of the SBE/curriculum link on campus is "block enrollment," in which a class in an academic subject (such as English) may contain students from only one vocational program (such as hospitality services or police science). This allows academic teachers to adapt a course to students' occupational interests and current SBE activities.

For students who wish to obtain a four-year degree, there is articulation with Ohio University, and a modified form of articulation occurs between Hocking and the high schools.

Two major programs illustrate the use of school-based enterprise at Hocking: the Wildlife Products enterprise and the sawmill. Wildlife Products makes birdfeeders and birdhouses in the college's woodworking shop. Students normally work ten hours a week on assignments that correspond to their majors: accounting students keep records, marketing students create advertisements, and so forth. Students doing physical production work get paid; the rest receive academic credit. Evaluation of students is done by the workshop instructor. Wildlife Products earns annual revenue of $34,000 to $39,000, which covers the cost of materials and students' wages.

Hocking has a broad and bold definition of school-based enterprise, and one of its bolder projects was the sawmill. Hocking used to have a "lumber" curriculum, which covered trading, drying, sawmilling, and other aspects of the industry. It took eight people just to operate the mill, which turned out 300,000 board feet a year with only three shifts per week. However, by 1991 enrollment was under fifteen students, so the program was terminated in 1992.

Hocking is committed to the concept of a business that educates rather than an educational system that teaches business. Teachers are encouraged to sell their expertise to the community. Special contracts with Jamaica and Argentina allow faculty to teach there. The mission statement is emphatic about the vocational nature of the school, and the teachers support it. Teachers are hired both to teach and to help run enterprises.

One staff person is assigned to help students start their own businesses. The college provides seed money for such ventures, and the staff person uses contacts on and off campus to assist the project. These enterprises help financially strapped students earn enough money to stay in school.

Hocking is a center for enterprise as much as for classroom teaching. It demonstrates that education through student employment can also contribute to community development. However, it takes clear commitment and a great deal of effort by the faculty and administration to make this combination succeed.

Gateway Technical College

In Kenosha, Wisconsin, Gateway Technical College operates a radio station as part of its two-year degree program in radio broadcasting. Students prepare for one of several entry-level occupations within the radio field: radio announcer (disc jockey, newscaster, sportscaster, or staff announcer), radio copywriter, or news writer/reporter.

Station KBLE is a for-profit SBE. It operates as a full-service radio station, providing live broadcasting from 7:00 A.M. to midnight five days a week while college is in session. The programming stresses alternative music: rock, blues, and jazz by new artists. The station is identified as an alternative radio station and does not compete with local commercial stations.

Students running the station take the roles of station manager, program director, production manager, sales manager, and promotions director. The team changes each semester. Students are encouraged to go on the air as soon as two months after starting.

The station earns income from several sources. Students sell and prepare commercials, which are then played as spots on the radio station. However, because of concern about competition with local radio stations, limited commercial spots are sold and the price is kept low — $.50 for a thirty-second spot and $1 for a sixty-second spot. This income is restricted to about $200 per year. Students also generate income by serving as disc jockeys and providing music at weddings, school dances, and other private parties. Twenty such events a year produce about $4,000. During the Christmas season, students create personalized Santa Claus tapes from the North Pole, which are a popu lar gift for young children. About fifty tapes were sold at $7.50 each in 1991. Profits from these entrepreneurial activities go into the treasury of the student organization and are used to repair and purchase equipment.

Enrollment in the 1992 program was twenty-two students — six second-year and sixteen first-year — and there have been as many as sixty students enrolled in previous years. The program usually graduates about twelve students each May. A recent follow-up study of graduates found that 70 percent were working full- or part-time at radio or television stations. The program also tracks students who drop out to take jobs in the industry. Nine out of ten of these reported that they were working in radio.

Station KBLE serves students all over the Gateway campus, not only those enrolled in the broadcasting course. While constrained from being aggressively competitive, the program exposes students to the full range of the station's operational issues.

PART TWO

The Benefits of
School-Based Enterprise

3

Teaching and Learning in a Practical Context

*E*ducation is the primary purpose of school-based enterprise in American high schools. This chapter describes how the productive activity of SBEs enables students to apply subject matter from the classroom, integrating academic and vocational knowledge as they learn many aspects of an industry. Productive activity also helps students develop their capacity for problem solving and time management and learn how to work in teams, how to learn through work, and how to participate in organizational redesign.

Learning Subject Matter from the Classroom

The teacher formerly in charge of the enterprise class at Mt. Edgecumbe explains how students' work there tied in with other classes:

> We had a number of cross-curricular projects that we were working on. Some ended up better than others. Of course, their math work was used over and over again within the class, doing statistical analysis. The Deming stuff was applied in a number

of different classes. English applied because of the different things that we had to write: the letters that had to be written, the records we had to keep, the tolerance limits and explanation of how to do our process. So we took a lot of what we were learning academically and applied it in that class in a way that made it important.

A telemarketing student at Hocking College testifies how composing scripts has improved her proficiency in English:

I've always [had] a hang-up about my English. Traveling around to so many schools, being an army child, I never felt I had proper grammar. So I have a real hang-up about that. When it came to writing scripts, I could talk on the telephone, talk in person, but writing the scripts I was scared to death. And so when I put them down, [the teacher] would point out to me, "This looks better if it's worded this way." And it's been great. I'm totally writing better in everything, just by being in the telemarketing lab learning how to write these scripts. All my writing that I'm doing in my other sales business management classes, letter writing, conversation on the telephone, and even conversation with people is improving by being in the telemarketing firm.

The mentorship program at Thomas Jefferson High School gives advanced students an opportunity to apply their classroom-based knowledge of science and technology to real problems in research firms and government laboratories. One participant expresses how exciting this is for her:

I got involved with it because I wanted the flexibility a mentorship offers. If you take senior tech lab, especially with the biotechnology department, you're really ushered through the whole program.

I had already taken a plant and tissue type course, so I wanted to do something that applied to what I had already learned, and learn more things, instead of just pretty much doing the same program over again. That's why I got involved with it, and I'm very glad that I did. The last day of school last year was my first day of work, and I worked all summer. It's an incredible experience. That's all I can say. I love it so much and am having a great time. They respect me like a member of the field.

The Mt. Edgecumbe enterprise teacher describes how requiring students to produce something makes learning more efficient because it puts students in the position of asking questions:

I give them the problem and they accept the problem as theirs. In this class [he currently teaches a marine science class, in which students are creating plans for a fish hatchery], they're one step beyond that. They not only accept the problem but they design the problem. They help design it. I give them the competencies they need to learn from doing the project, and then together we make sure that it matches. Then I make the knowledge available. I just tell them, "Here's a book: you can look in this book for it. You can look in such and such encyclopedias in the library." Sometimes I have videos. And then I say, "I'll just tell you, if you want to listen, the background information you need to know to do this project." Well, basically it's a lot of the same material that I would give them anyway, but what I've found is that if you put the knowledge first and the lecture first, if you try to feed them all the information first, no one wants to listen. Before, the way I was doing it, I was trying to give them the information, and they always fought me tooth and nail. You know, kids would fall asleep, kids would be fighting, kids would be talking. I'd be spending my whole time trying to get people focused. Whereas now, they have the problem, they need the knowledge, they ask you questions. Before, they tried not to ask questions because that would make the lecture longer. Now, they'll be so intent that you can cover in forty-five minutes what might have taken you a whole week before to do. And they'll accept it. They'll write the information down, and then they'll go and apply it. They have to apply the information they get, so they remember it.

Despite the potential advantages of learning through productive projects, there is sometimes skepticism from students, faculty, and the community, especially if the projects take students out of the classroom during regular school hours. For example, students in the Belle Fourche creative writing course were preparing a local history that they were going to publish and sell. The instructor describes some initial negative responses: "'What are those kids doing on school time down here?' [a local merchant asked.] Faculty wondered, 'Why aren't [students] in their classes?' It was about four years of some real unpleasantness." The teacher of the research-and-development course at Belle Fourche describes that initial resistance and some of the effort to overcome it:

In terms of the faculty, there were some problems just getting people to understand that classrooms don't necessarily have four walls. Because, of course, in the research-and-development course, when you're trying to operate the business out here, and you're trying to meet with community people downtown, and you're organizing a dinner theater and going grocery shopping, you know our kids were seldom in the classroom. They were running all over, so they were in the halls a lot. It took a little bit of education so that the faculty got used to that. We also had some explaining to do in the community. When suddenly you have somebody walking into your place of business at 1:30 in the afternoon when they're supposed to be in school, there are some explanations to be made for that.

But I think we've done a pretty good job in the community. I think the community really understands that. In fact, Linda does a publication, "A Classroom Without Walls," and all of that was an attempt to get the whole idea, even if nothing more than in the title of the publication, into the community so that they had more of an idea of what we were all about.

Integrating Academic and Vocational Education

In addition to applying information and concepts from academic courses, many SBEs, rooted in vocational education, are directly concerned with work-related knowledge and skill. Recently, however, there is renewed interest in combining vocational and academic education, and SBEs can serve as vehicles for this integration.

The 1917 Smith-Hughes Act first authorized federal money for vocational education and established it as a distinct field of instruction within American high schools. However, in 1990 Congress decreed that federal funds for vocational education must henceforward be spent only on programs that integrate academic and vocational education. The hope is that such integration will improve vocational instruction by raising the level of academic skill and knowledge involved and at the same time improve academic instruction by demonstrating more practical applications.

The SBE at Mt. Edgecumbe exemplifies this dual purpose. The superintendent explains how he conceived the SBE as a vehicle for preparing students to make a living as well as teaching academic subjects:

My theory of learning is that you should have project-oriented classes. You should use cross-curricular approaches. Everything should be integrated or intertwined. So I started thinking, "How can you mesh Pacific Rim with vocational education? Well, why not set up an export business? Also, if you set up the export business, doesn't that then include the Pacific Rim cultures class that we require all of our kids to take? Wouldn't it also include Japanese or Chinese or Russian?" They all have to take a foreign language here, one of those three. Why not make the language real? So we did it. We set it up as a business whose primary focus initially was to export salmon to Japan.

It took us about a year and a half to get everything set up. And then we started to do labels. That involved art classes. It also had to involve the Japanese language class, because they had to do the Japanese labels. If you look at my business card, it's got Japanese on the back of it. They did all those business cards. We just started integrating everything we could. The math teacher had to start converting yen to dollars, ounces to grams. We require two years of computers here for our kids. Well, that fits into this whole model, because if you've got a computer background, you can do spreadsheets and you can do some of these other things. So the computer teachers become a part of this team too.

At the time of our visit, Edgecumbe Enterprises was in transition. The new project will continue to combine academic and vocational pursuits, as the superintendent envisions:

Now you're right in the throes of it. This is going on right now. We advertised in the paper that our school was interested in working with a local business on value-added products. We had two proposals turned in. The kids had the people come in and talk to them. Then they selected the company they wanted to go with. It's Sitka Sound Seafoods. So what the plan is now — this is the one that's going through my mind, and I haven't sat down and brainstormed all of this yet with the other teachers — but what I'd like is to take our computer teacher and take some of his kids out of computer II class. I'd like to take our Pacific Rim teacher, who also teaches Japanese, and our algebra II teacher, and I'd like to get kids from each of those classes, probably three or four kids from each class. I'd like to form a class then for the second semester. And what we'd do then is a retail business setup for Sitka Sound Seafoods. They need research done, and they need product development, etc. And then the other thing they want to do, while they're setting up their retail outlet to get ready for next summer's tourist season, is set up a catalog operation. So what I want our kids to do is to end up with a Japanese catalog, a Chinese catalog, a Russian catalog. Some groups will be working on that, depending on the expertise of the kids, while other kids are working on product development. This will be the entrepreneurship class. They'll start testing products for the company, which they're doing right now. They're running sample kipper products through there right now. We've got to look at crab. We're looking at smoked mussels, possibly smoked clams. There are all kind of different things that they may be able to market that are readily available right here. We're in a paradise as far as seafood is concerned right here.

The computer class at Mt. Edgecumbe plays a crucial part in bridging different classes; teachers and students exploit the computer's versatility as both a vocational and academic tool. One student tells with relish how she used her computer skills to produce a business plan (one of the requirements in the entrepreneurship class):

I did a computer report on my projection, my business projection, and that went to computer II as extra credit for my personal profile project [a life-planning exercise]. We were coming up with a personal business thing which kind of hooked right into that at the time. I don't think the teachers talked about it, but it came in really handy with me: "I've already got my plan. Here, I'll pull out my table. How I plan to do it and where I'm going to be." So I used Microsoft Excel, put my business plan on Microsoft Word 4.0, typed it up, did all my calculations, turned it in. Bound it up, turned it in, and said, "Here it is."

Other connections between the work in SBEs and academic subjects are also apparent. The link between telemarketing and English composition has already been mentioned, and there is also an obvious tie between telemarketing and speech. And a student in the flower shop on the Metro Tech campus mentions how she uses math: "We're learning to price things. We're pricing things in our heads: how much our designs are worth."

Because school-based enterprise combines academic and vocational knowledge, it can help students prepare for college and beyond, as indicated by a student in the Fairfax Classroom on the Mall: "I've been in this program for three years. I think when I put that on a college application, it's going to show some kind of commitment. I think it's going to help me out. And it's going to help me in a job after college, even if it's not related to fashion or marketing."

At the other end of the achievement spectrum, school-based enterprise provides a context in which students who resist regular classroom instruction are willing to sit still for a limited amount of theoretical instruction. The principal of the construction program in Fairfax County says,

[We] usually try to run theory in inclement situations. When it's too cold or it's raining, you can't work outside. Then you do your theory work. You can't sit a student down and do theory for three hours. It's a problem, because they're not going to sit there that long. Do thirty to forty minutes of the-

ory and get them out working. If it's raining outside, take them out there and get them all wet, then
come back in and they'll sit there and listen to you.
If you're going to let them sit in there for two days,
you might as well take a gun and blow your own
brains out.

At Hocking College, the block scheduling of students for
SBE and other technical classes has influenced the academic
classes to focus on related themes. An administrator explains:

> What happens is, you're a teacher of sociology and,
> bingo, in come fourteen of your twenty students
> who are police science majors. Where do you think
> the discussion is going in that class? You have French
> the same way. So what you have is these people
> coming through the system with the technical driv-
> ing the scheduling process. When you do that, the
> instructors create their classes to relate to the stu-
> dents. The department director will give the instruc-
> tor the same kind of schedule each term and, lo and
> behold, the instructor gets the same kind of students
> each time and ends up building the class. In terms
> of enterprise, where that comes in: if a student says,
> "I'm working at the Lodge [Hocking's college-owned
> hotel] next week, and my job is to supervise the
> housekeeping department," and you have to write
> a theme, the theme topics that are given out in that
> class — very likely there would be five topics, and
> one might be, "What would you say to a person
> in the hotel business who has a problem?" So the
> infusion of the enterprise into the person creates
> an infusion of the enterprise into the general-studies
> program.

These examples illustrate that when schoolwork is grounded
in a practical context, students' desire to solve problems arising
from that context gives a pragmatic meaning to all subjects and
makes the boundaries between them less important.

Learning Multiple Aspects of an Industry

Traditional vocational education has too often restricted its aim to teaching specific skills and knowledge required in entry-level jobs. This has reduced the appeal of vocational education to students who aspire (and whose parents aspire for them) to managerial or professional occupations. The level of academic performance expected on the part of students in traditional vocational education has also too often been correspondingly low. To correct these problems, the 1990 amendments to the Carl D. Perkins Vocational and Applied Technology Education Act contained repeated directions that vocational classes should teach "all aspects of the industry." School-based enterprise readily lends itself to this purpose.

For example, at Coop Tech's construction site in New York City, students do a wider range of jobs than they ordinarily would with commercial contractors. Students take part in demolition, framing, masonry, plumbing, electrical work, finished carpentry, tile setting, and sheetrocking. (The SBE construction experience also potentially involves students in reading blueprints and estimating costs.) In contrast, one student, who had held an after-school job in a department store "just doing stock," complained, "You can't learn anything from stacking those boxes, except how to put them in one straight shape, up and down."

SBEs often give students responsibility for dealing with costs and prices. Telemarketing students at Hocking College help determine how much to charge per call. Marketing students in Fairfax County's Classroom on the Mall are given a budget (an "open to buy") to acquire merchandise, for which they then decide the selling price. A student describes the process: "We all get together and we just look at what we think would sell, what we all like. We usually have different opinions, but we work something out. We take the regular price of what it costs for us to buy it, and we usually double that. It depends on what it is. But then if we think they're not going to pay that much, we'll take it down. Get a price in between there. That's the good thing about this program. We do it all ourselves, basically."

Another aspect of real enterprise with which students contend in the Classroom on the Mall is shoplifting. This fascinates students, according to the teacher. "One unit that we always do is the shoplifting-prevention unit. The director of security [for the mall] comes and talks to them. It's always a riveting unit. They're always very interested, very curious. I think just because it's risky and, at that age, that's an interesting topic for them."

Handling money is an aspect with which students in most retail SBEs deal, within limits. The instructor in the Rothsay store explains their daily procedure: "The students will be closing the store. They'll then take all of the cash out of the register, place it in the safe box. The next morning is when the till is checked out. They go through and we start each day with $49.50 cash in the till. All slips and so forth are then taken in, and the accounting process is started. The students reconcile the detail tape against the sales slips and then count the cash." However, students themselves do not close out the cash register; that is done by an adult employee. Similarly, for legal reasons, "Our students cannot write checks. We don't make bank deposits, so they don't know how to make the deposits, but we'll go across to the bank and get change and so forth. We can't do the school's bookwork. That's why I say they'll get the 80 [percent of what there is to learn], but they can't get the other 20 because it's impossible, I think."

Job rotation is used in some SBEs to ensure that students learn all parts of the operation — sometimes against a student's own wishes. Rotation is central to the culinary program at Metro Tech, for example:

> We just divide [entering students] up equally among the three stations: front service, bake shop, kitchen. And then every week we rotate them. They rotate within the stations. So they'll rotate through all the kitchen jobs and then rotate out into the bake shop. Go through all the bake shop jobs, rotate out, go into front service. Usually we put them in pairs. If we have a lot of students, we put two or three

students per job. If we're really low, then it could just be one. It depends on our population. But we want the student to experience all three stations. A lot of times you'll find a student who will say, "Well, I just want to do kitchen. I don't want to do anything else," or "I just want to be in bake shop" or "I just want to be a waiter." But we still want them to be exposed to all three stations. And then second semester, I go ahead and let the kid specialize. I'd rather have him be happy in a station that he wants to be in than lose him. Because I've had students come to me and say, "You know, if you put me in bake shop, I'm dropping the program." Well, in order to keep them, I'll keep them in the kitchen or front service or wherever they want to be.

The commitment to letting students learn all aspects of the industry is also explicit at Mt. Edgecumbe. The superintendent declares, "If there are a hundred things that these kids need to know about how you get a product ready to market, they're going to learn them here. And if there are a hundred things you need to know about what to do with the product after you've got it ready to market, they're all going to learn those things." As an example, because Edgecumbe Enterprises is licensed as a business and is therefore inspected for compliance with health and safety regulations, students become familiar with that regulatory process.

While the entrepreneurship class at Mt. Edgecumbe does the actual product development and marketing, processes and packages the fish, and deals with ongoing production issues, the business applications class is responsible for financial management and strategic planning. Students in that class maintain a balance sheet and produce monthly profit-and-loss statements using computerized spreadsheets. They also make sales tax payments. The business applications class performs these services not only for the fish-processing enterprise but also for the school newspaper, the student-body company, and other campus organizations.

In 1990–91 students in the business applications class constituted the class as a board of directors for Edgecumbe Enterprises. Students produced a book of policies and procedures that contains a vision statement, a strategic plan for the following year, and descriptions of the responsibilities of each officer, among other things. A review of minutes of the board meetings reveals that students routinely discuss a wide range of issues. Labor-management relations, for example, were a matter of concern on at least one occasion: the minutes for February 6, 1991, record that the chief executive officer complained, "We're not communicating with [the entrepreneurship class] at all. There are kids that aren't taking it seriously, some of them that just don't care."

The teacher who originally taught the entrepreneurship class describes how students grappled with this issue:

> It's tedious work doing the same thing. Repetitive work. One thing we did was rotate so that one person didn't spend one semester operating the slicer and one person operating the vacuum-packaging machine, though in regular business I think they would do that a lot. Our students said if we had a business we would rotate also, because that would help cut down on the boring aspect of it. And people will have good ideas. If they operate the slicer, they may have a really good idea about how to put fish onto the package. They rotated daily. That was one of their ideas.

Entrepreneurship students did extensive test-marketing of various smoked salmon products. One former student recalls,

> A lot of people came here testing the fish, and the student body tested it too. We had teachers, staff members, everybody tasted it. We said, "Okay, here are comment sheets. We want you to write your comments. What would make it better? What could make it more inviting to you to come in and buy

it?" So the students would say, "Okay, a little less on the salt because it's too salty." Or the Japanese would say it was too cooked because they like their stuff raw. So we take that and combine it and say, "Okay, this is just like a business, like Motorola. They got the quality prize. They get comments from everybody. They ask their customers what makes their product so important and successful." Then we'd relate it back to fish.

This student is one of about two dozen who have traveled from Mt. Edgecumbe to Japan, in part to investigate the market for smoked salmon. "I never saw any products exactly like ours," she says, "but I saw some things similar. And I took down a lot of ideas of what I saw there. I said, 'Okay, here's our audience; here's what they want: refrigeration in these countries is expensive, so they can't have big packages.' If we were going to target our audience to people in Japan, we have to make a small product."

The superintendent explains how these remarkable marketing excursions came about.

We went in 1987, 1989, and 1991. The contact over there was a group called Alaska Kai, which means "great committee." It's a nonprofit organization in Japan that promotes import and export business as well as education. What they were looking for was some kind of marriage that could be made with a school that was serious about dealing with Japan, and serious in dealing in a quality manner, serious enough to have Japanese language, Pacific Rim cultures. All the things we were doing fit exactly what they thought should be happening in a school.

They meet you in Narita [the Tokyo airport], and they take care of you. The normal stay is fifteen days, and they take care of everything. I went over in 1989, and I was treated like a king. I couldn't believe what they did. They even took us on vacation for two days. They said, "We want to show you how the Japanese people have vacation," so they sent us to the beach in condos. What we asked them to do was not give us the normal tour. What we want to do is take these kids to meet with businesspeople, not bureaucrats and educators. We want to go to the Tokyo fish market. We want to go to actual fish plants, see product development. We want to see what's being sold, what's being processed.

We ended up with CEOs of major Japanese fish corporations, seafood corporations. We brought over samples of our products. We had them critiqued. One CEO brought in his two top people. We sat around in this plush office with these two young Japanese girls who came in and took our product and placed it on plates, and we went through a whole sampling thing. Texture, appearance — they went through everything. They chewed us out because we had different size packages. The height of your product can't be so many centimeters from the top and so many centimeters from the sides, and each one of them has to be exactly the same. The thickness of the cut has to be exactly the same on each cut. You can't have any fish oil leaking through the back of the product. So we came back here and boy did we redo things! We redid them to their standards. But you talk about kids learning — now that's the real world!

The superintendent and faculty at Mt. Edgecumbe feel that students can learn a great deal from running a productive enterprise, dealing with the problems that arise, and constantly trying to improve. But after a while, the opportunities for learning diminish. Then it is time to start something new. When we visited Mt. Edgecumbe in the fall of 1991, the entrepreneurship class was in the early phases of developing a new product. The new teacher explains:

Next semester this program will go even deeper into product development. We'll be utilizing other courses — science and business applications. This semester we're concentrating on product development and process. This class is a processing class, but the emphasis has always been on how to develop a product. We have the products that we've developed in the past, and we still are going to be doing some of that. Originally, we were going to do the lox and walk this class through the process, but it very quickly became evident that that was not the highest value in the class. It would be better for them to get into product development on their own. That's where the value is.

The value of product development is both economic and educational: it contributes to regional development by demonstrating new ways to add value to natural seafood resources before exporting them, and it exposes students to the multiple aspects of the industry that must be considered when starting something new.

Problem Solving

What students learn from school-based enterprise extends beyond understanding a particular industry, important as that is. A much more far-reaching benefit is the development of students' competence and confidence in problem solving. The former entrepreneurship teacher at Mt. Edgecumbe, currently teaching marine science, comments on the gains from orienting instruction around a productive project:

We're involved in a statewide project to design a submersible robot to go to Prince William Sound and sample the bottom for what's left of the oil spill and see if there's still an impact. These students have been working for a couple of weeks. They've written an explanation of how this vehicle is going to work. They have drawings that they've done on the computer to explain how they want it to look — different views: rear view, bottom view, top view. This project meets some of the competencies that we have to do for the year in marine science. Very similar to what we do in entrepreneurship, where doing the project meets the needs of understanding how to run a business. It comes from our philosophy that students should *do* things. We want to create students who can do things, not necessarily students who have this large body of knowledge. The Trivial Pursuit type of student is not as valuable to us as someone who can actually do something like this.

A student in telemarketing at Hocking College describes the kind of problems she has had to contend with:

We have customer complaints. A person's out in San Francisco. He says his Rocky Boots leaked. "Well, how long have you had your boots, sir?" "I've had them since Christmas, but I haven't worn them yet," or "I got them last Christmas as a gift and I've worn them only twice and they leak." "Well, you could take them back to the store, sir." "Well, I got them as a gift, and I don't know where the person got the boots." They all want to send their boots back to the factory to have them replaced, because they don't want to go back to the retailer, or they've gone back to the retailer who doesn't want anything more to do with the boots. So students need to learn how to finesse customers. Sometimes you have to learn how to say no to customers, think on your feet, and make some judgments about those kinds of things.

Although most telemarketing interactions are based on a script, improvisation is often necessary:

Basically, in our script we have something to respond with. If we don't, the way we handle it is very simple and it satisfies them immensely: "Would you please hold a minute while I check with my supervisor?" Very easily done, and whether you have a supervisor or not, you can collect your thoughts on that problem. I've done that many times, because that person knows you're going to take the time to find out the right answer, and maybe you just had to think about what the right answer was, but you can put them on hold and get a good answer together and come back.

Since the SBE is an educational setting, students are not expected to know all the answers. When they cannot improvise a solution, the teacher can help out. Again the telemarketing student illustrates:

We had a poor man who was really furious about not being able to make a toll-free call to a representative of the shoe company. He was belligerent and went on and on about money and that he'd have to pay for this phone call and he wanted these shoes and on and on, and no matter what I said, no matter what I recommended, no matter what I did, he wasn't going to give up. One student said, "Why don't you just hang up?" You just don't do that. You try to satisfy the customer. So I put him on hold, and I went over to [the teacher] and I said, "I can't get anywhere with him. He's not satisfied; he doesn't want to call the sales rep." [The teacher] said, "Get the man's name and phone number. We'll call the sales rep, and the rep can call the man back." I didn't feel I had the power to do that. Now I feel comfortable using that approach in other situations.

Child care is another area that poses problems that can be extremely serious in an SBE, requiring teachers to help students. For example, a teacher in the Brooks County child-care center recounts, "If Susie took a baby to the bathroom to change a diaper and she saw that she had bruises on her — and that's happened — then Susie would go tell the teacher's aide. That person would probably tell one of us, and we would have to call and be responsible."

Students at Coop Tech likewise receive on-the-spot instruction as they encounter problems in renovating an old six-story brick building. For example, replacing old beams is a major undertaking, and it is crucial to get them level. The beams are cemented into the brick-bearing wall, and it is difficult to jimmy them out in order to replace or reset them. The instructors teach sometimes by explaining, sometimes by wordless demonstration. One student remembers, "One day, I was like, 'Mr. [teacher], the beam's not staying straight.' I see him put in this nail. He doesn't explain; I'm just there looking. Like, 'Oh, so that's it.' Afterward I tried it one day, and it worked." Seeing how the teacher solved the problem enabled the student subsequently to solve it on his own.

The process for teaching students to solve problems on their own can be informal and haphazard or formal and deliberate. Mt. Edgecumbe exemplifies the formal approach. Systematic procedures for improving quality are used throughout the instructional program, including the SBE. The former teacher of the entrepreneurship class explains how the problem-solving procedure worked:

> We collected statistics on a large number of our processes, and we applied the Deming methodology to problem solving. When we had a problem, we'd form a team. The team would collect data on the problem. Then they would brainstorm possible solutions. They'd pick one solution, make a plan, do the fix. Then they'd collect data to see if the problem was fixed.

One former student gives an example of how they applied continuous problem solving:

> Before we even started class, we said, "What's the problem with this?" so that people would have an

idea of what to expect and what problems. One problem would be the smell of fish. There's no way that we can get rid of that. We're stuck with it. But there's something we can do: get gloves. You don't have to have your hands smell if you wear gloves. [The teacher] said, "Well, okay, we'll get gloves." Here's another problem: what about health regulations, hair safety? Okay, hairnets. Let's work on that. And so everybody was required to get hairnets and gloves and wear an apron.

But this led to another problem:

Hairnets and gloves all over the processing room. That was because the students were irresponsible about putting them away. We had group team members. They started on the project, and they said, "Okay, here's our problem area right here. This isn't working, so from here on we need to find something that's going to work." So they came up with what the solution was. The solution was we can make a little rack to put them on.

This solution was reached after other proposed solutions had been rejected. One proposal that was discarded was having the gloves and hairnets stacked in a container on the shelf. "We thought that would be kind of unsanitary, because the hairnets are personalized." The idea of zipper plastic bags pasted on the wall was also rejected, "because the zipper bags fall apart, and they're not reliable." The idea that was finally implemented was a board, with "nails in every couple of inches and a clothesline clip nailed in there. So all they had to do is just pinch that and put their gloves in and their hairnet over it." After this action was taken, the effects were studied by the student problem-solving team.

They may have a little chart that said, like maybe it's 10/6/90, hairnets found in room, and then the gloves, how many pairs of gloves. And then they'd say, "Okay, here we found six," and they put a little frown on it. And then the next time they found one other, so that would be another frown. Then one day everybody hung their stuff and was responsible, so there would be a big smiley face there. And they said, "Okay, this is working, but not to the extent we wanted it to." So they kept doing the process on that. . . . It keeps going around and around. It doesn't stop.

Other problems subjected to the continual problem-solving process at Mt. Edgecumbe were how to clean the fish smoker without making a big mess, how to arrange the equipment to minimize wasted motion in processing, how to increase awareness of Edgecumbe Enterprises in the town of Sitka, and how to keep improving the brine (in which fish are soaked before smoking) and smoking times to produce better-tasting kippers and lox.

The payoff from mastering this problem-solving process is evident not only in the SBE but also in other areas of students' lives. One student told us that applying this process enabled her to solve the problem of how to find time and space to do her homework, and she had heard of students who used this process to work on the biggest problem of all: what to do with their lives after high school. They implemented plans that they had conceived in the entrepreneurship class. "They had visions and goals, and a couple of students actually did do their goals. I think they're down in the lower forty-eight [states]. They planned it out and they got funding for everything, and they're paying off and they're doing really well."

Time Management

Because most SBEs operate in blocks of time that are larger than ordinary class periods, and often at different times than regular school hours, students involved must learn to budget their time. As the principal at Thomas Jefferson High School notes, having to spend fifteen or twenty hours a week off campus at a mentorship site limits the amount of time students have available for extracurricular school activities and personal social activities, including family events. Thomas Jefferson students themselves report loss of sleep and study time because of long work hours and extra commute time, loss of opportunity to participate in extracurricular school activities and to enroll in elective classes, and loss of contact with family and friends because of the mentorship time commitments and responsibilities. And many students participating in the mentorship program hold other jobs on weekends or in the evening; these responsibilities further reduce their discretionary time. Similar problems are encountered by students in several other SBEs — for example, the Classroom on the Mall in Fairfax County and the Rothsay store, which remain open in the late afternoon and evening, on Saturdays, and (in the case of Rothsay) during the nonschool summer months.

One student who developed his own business as a result of his experience in the entrepreneurship activity in Belle Fourche reports, "I've gotten to the point where I have to schedule people in my little datebook: to see your friend So-and-so." A student enrolled in a cosmetology SBE away from her home talks about the cost of her involvement in the program: "My senior year in high school I gave up a lot of my friends; I gave up lots of my high school experiences." Another student in this same program echoes that point: "My senior year in high school — everything, all of the activities." Taking on the commitment to be part of a school enterprise requires that students set priorities and manage time carefully.

Teamwork

More than conventional classes, and more than placements in jobs outside the school, SBEs provide a structure for students to learn how to work in teams. Sometimes the work simply cannot be done by one person alone — for example, the hoisting of a steel I beam on the Coop Tech construction site. Teachers in the Coop Tech construction project have taken advantage of the natural necessity for teamwork by dividing the students into crews of five, each headed by a crew leader. At the beginning of the work day, the teacher in charge gives directions to the crew leaders, who then relay them to the crews. According to one of the teachers, crew leaders "have got to learn to delegate a bit, and to share, and to think about it, without creating dissension."

At the Fairfax County car-repair enterprise, the orientation for students includes teamwork exercises. One student recalls, "We had a puzzle we had to put together at the beginning of the year showing that you can't do something by yourself as well as you can do something with other people. If you work together well, you get it done faster and right." The lesson, as another student puts it, is "that you are all running the dealership together, and if you don't get along together, the dealership is not going to be successful."

Fairfax County's Classroom on the Mall was experimenting with a new team incentive structure when we studied it. Students were grouped into four departments, responsible for seasonal soft goods, nonseasonal soft goods, seasonal hard goods, and nonseasonal hard goods. Various aspects of each team's performance were rated, and at the end of the year the winning team was taken out to lunch. This confronted students with the problem of how to deal with team members who do not pull their own weight. According to one student,

> I noticed that some people in our group didn't take the shoplifting program seriously, and some of us had to therefore take their load and do it. We like the idea of working in groups and doing competition, but depending on somebody else for our [performance rating] — we didn't really like that part. But they also gave us individual grades, so that kind of made up for it. We were supposed to meet at my house one evening to type up our whole thing, and some people didn't show up. Only one of the girls that didn't show called and said she couldn't show up. She did hers on her own at home. There-

fore it was ready for us the next day so we could
just put it in our booklet. The other people, we had
to think what was their part, and we had to totally
write up their part and then type it up and put it
in the booklet because my team, we're really big
on everything has to be perfect.

Teamwork in some SBEs includes the expectation that
students will teach each other. The instructor in charge of Southington's school store describes one such arrangement: "At the
beginning of the year, the seniors break in the juniors. The first
half of the year, we're running different junior kids through the
store. The seniors teach them how to ring [sales on the register],
all that they need to do in terms of stocking and pricing—that
kind of stuff. Usually during the second half of the year the
juniors start operating and the seniors start losing interest. We
train the kids in change, marking, tallying, how to talk to the
customers. There's also a training manual that we use."

Students are responsible for teaching each other at Mt.
Edgecumbe too. This idea actually emerged from one of the
problem-solving groups studying the number of students who
did and did not know how to do each task. According to the
former teacher,

They devised a system where, if the student didn't
know, they went to the student manager and then,
if the manager didn't know, the manager would
come to me. First they were supposed to ask other
students nearby how to do it if they didn't know.
They found it would be more efficient to get help
from another student first if they could. And then
if that student couldn't help them, they'd go to the
manager, who'd been in the program for two years.
And then if that didn't work, they'd come to me.
They realized that if they came to me they may have
to wait, because I might be solving another problem at the time or doing something else.

The quality of teamwork itself becomes a subject for analysis at Mt. Edgecumbe. A student relates how one discussion raised the issue of unequal commitment to quality standards by SBE members:

> The teacher says, "Okay, today we did a lot of work, but there also was a lot of arguing. What was the cause of it? What can we do to change it and make it better?" I said, "Well, the person that was slicing wasn't very careful, and they almost sliced their finger." That's possible. It's really dangerous. And I said the people that do slicing should be paying more attention. I brought that up. And we got into an argument, but I said, "I'm doing this because the product you're producing affects me, because I'm on this line. I have my name signed to this just as much as you do."

Identification with the work makes this student feel responsible for her teammates.

Lave and Wenger (1991) view learning as a social process. In other words, people learn through participation in a community of practice. The superintendent at Mt. Edgecumbe believes that the sense of purposeful community provides the supporting social "infrastructure" necessary for students to do their academic best. He describes the reaction of visitors from other schools:

> [They] spend a couple of days here and they say, "You know, I don't see that much difference between what you're doing and what we're doing, but what I don't understand is, How come your kids have such a different attitude? How come they like to learn? And how come they're back here on these computers every night? There are all kinds of cooperative learning taking place. How do you get your kids to do twenty to twenty-five hours of home-

work a week? We can't get our kids to do any home-
work. How do you get them to turn in projects?
How do you get them to turn in quality projects?
How do you get them to write?"

He answers, "If you're not feeling good about yourself, and the
infrastructure isn't in place to allow all of those things, then the
other things can't take place."

In the small Alaskan school district where the superintendent worked prior to Mt. Edgecumbe, the instructional pro-
gra ̇ ˑ was successful in raising students' test scores and getting
them into college, but many of the college students came home
within a few weeks. "I couldn't figure out what was going on.
What was the piece missing? We were academically preparing
those kids. It wasn't our fault. It must have been the parents'
fault. It couldn't have been our fault. Then I got here, and I
realized the piece that was missing. You also have to take care
of the whole social aspect of that kid as well as the academic."

Pervasive use of teamwork, embedding each student's
effort in a larger group, provides social support along with academic preparation, allowing Mt. Edgecumbe students not only
to reach college but also to stay there. In January of 1991, a
Mt. Edgecumbe survey of 179 graduates from the classes of 1986
through 1990 found 62 of them — or 35 percent — enrolled in four-
year colleges or universities. Seven more were in two-year colleges
or postsecondary vocational schools, and 10 had graduated from
postsecondary vocational schools. Evidently the project-based,
team-learning strategy at Mt. Edgecumbe helps students build
the capacity and confidence for continued academic pursuits.

Generic Work Skills

The intellectual and social competence developed through participation in school-based enterprise prepares students not only
for further education but also for their eventual work. Teachers
emphasize generic work skills, starting with the importance of
showing up for work. An instructor in one of the school restaurants declares, "If they have poor attendance, that means that

on the job, they're going to do the same thing. So a chef's not going to hire. You miss one day in this business, the chef says, 'There's the door.'" Other necessary behaviors mentioned by this instructor include being on time and "staying on task at what they're doing. That's part of the responsibility. And if they can't do it here, there's no way they're going to make it on the outside."

In a similar vein, an instructor at the Fairfax County car dealership explains, "What we teach them is not just that pistons go up and down and spark plugs fire. We teach them a lot about job responsibilities, common courtesy, work ethics." A student in this program confirms that emphasis: "He grades us each day on attendance, on how well we work throughout the day, even on how well we clean up afterwards. Attendance is like 10 percent, cleanup is like 10 percent. Your actual classwork is probably like 75 percent."

Other generic work skills are described by the teacher in charge of the telemarketing center at Hocking College.

> I tell them this: the value we add to your education at this center has to do with communication. The students have poor communication skills when they come, and they've improved them a great deal. . . . By having to talk to people on the phone, the students learn some of those communication skills. When I hear a student say, "We ain't got no," I scream at them, "Don't tell a customer, 'We ain't got no'; that's bad grammar!" Most students don't say that, but I'm using that as a blatant example. But the other thing we do is teach students to think on their feet, and so much of going to college is "This is what the professor said, that I put in my notebook; this is what I put on a test." Now, how do you think on your feet? What I tell students is that you'll have to make that decision, that's one of those decisions you'll have to make every day in business, every day you pick up the phone, every day you deal with a customer, a client. When is enough enough? When do you tell a customer you're

finished? Sometimes there's a logical conclusion, but sometimes you're going to have to tailor the script.

At Coop Tech, where the wages students are paid may be their first regular income, teachers advise them on how to manage money:

> We try to explain to them; we call their stipend a paycheck. "You get your paycheck. You have to allot a certain amount. You need new work boots. You lost your hammer; you've got to get it replaced. It'll cost you X number of dollars to replace it. You have to allot that from your paycheck." You know, giving them survival skills. It's what it comes down to — you know, reality. We've been around for a bit, so we're familiar with it. Every one of us has done our time in industry somewhere along the line, and we know there are certain things: you need work clothes; it costs X number of dollars. You get a paycheck for $98, you can't go out and party Saturday and blow the whole thing, you know. You have to put a certain amount away.

Leadership is another issue given explicit attention at Coop Tech. As we have noted, students in the construction project are divided into five-person crews, each with a student leader. A teacher describes how he has tried to help one crew leader develop leadership ability:

> The kid has an attention deficit. He really does. He tries; I mean, you know, he's not a slacker, by any means. He has an attention deficit. But he can work with certain kids. He can't work with others because he's very, um . . . I'm trying to think of a word for it: very outspoken with what he wants. Some of the kids can't take that kind of direction. We pulled some kids out of his crew and changed a couple of crews around. A kid who's more fragile

can't deal with him. They become fearful. So okay,
we see that and shift them. You know, we do what
we can to accommodate the kids.

Some of these generic work skills are the kinds of capacities described by the Secretary's Commission on Achieving
Necessary Skills (the SCANS commission) in *What Work Requires of Schools* (U.S. Department of Labor, 1991). At Mt. Edgecumbe, for example, students learn basic concepts of quality
control in production systems. They also learn a range of in-
terpersonal skills, including how to present themselves and their
achievements. One former student in the enterprise class describes some of what she got out of it:

> Our only work was to show up and basically par-
> ticipate and just understand your goals of what
> you're doing and why you're doing it. And be able
> to tell somebody else, "I'm competent in this area
> because not only do I know the knowledge of it — I
> can take a test and pass it — but also I can analyze
> it, take it apart, explain it. I can apply it to new
> ideas and I can appreciate it because I've gotten
> results and I've done stuff and here's what I've
> done." You can walk into an employer and say,
> "This is what I've done. This is what I'm capable
> of. Here's my hardware." You know, like your
> disks. "Here are my disks, my hard copy, and what
> I'm able to achieve." And you know you can show
> that to a boss and say, "This is why I'm good for
> this, because I've got competency skills in this level
> of this thing." And I think that's impressive when
> you can go in to see somebody and say, "Hey, I
> know what I'm doing because here I am."

This student envisioned a conversation with a prospective employer as a two-way street. She felt prepared to size up potential employers, because the enterprise class had taught her
"the operational definition of what a business is. I can go up

to a business and ask the right questions: 'What's your job here? Why are you here? And what are you going to do with it? Are you going places, and what's your vision?' If you can ask a business that and get the answers you want back — you've got to be able to ask the right questions or you're wasting time."

One of the most important generic work skills in a fast-changing economy is knowing how to use work as a learning experience. Since SBE is intended to do exactly that, students become aware of the learning process and are able to talk about it. For example, a Coop Tech student talks about learning to use a saw, where results are tangible: "When you see you can cut better than what you first cut, that's when you know you learned." A telemarketing student at Hocking College reflects on the benefit of being "cast to the wolves": "You can make your learning experience by your mistakes, and you don't forget what you're learning that way." These students are self-consciously practicing how to learn from their own work experience.

They are also learning how to participate in the design and redesign of organizations for the twin purposes of education and production. Students creating new ventures in Rothsay and Belle Fourche are involved in thinking through new organizational arrangements. The crews at Coop Tech, the experimental "departments" in the Fairfax Classroom on the Mall, and the self-analytic teams at Mt. Edgecumbe are all grappling with the question of how best to organize their efforts in order to get the work done and learn as much as possible from doing it. This is the same question facing nonschool enterprises in a market environment where innovation and continuous improvement are increasingly important. SBE students are preparing to participate in work organizations that must continually reinvent themselves.

Specific Work Skills

Last but not least, students in SBEs acquire knowledge and skills for which they can immediately be paid in the workplace. Since many SBEs are attached to vocational programs, there are lists of specific work competencies that students are expected to achieve. At the Fairfax County car dealership, for example, the instructor affirms that students "learn transferable skills and earn a certificate of achievement in a specialized field, experience a realistic production-oriented auto-dealership operation, and participate in adopt-a-school opportunities provided by local auto retailers." In the Coop Tech construction project, students obtain at least rudimentary knowledge of techniques ranging from safe demolition procedures to setting ceramic bathroom tile. The director of the culinary program at Hocking College claims, "If you were to interview employers of our graduates, they would tell you that the students who make it through the program are able to withstand the pressure of the work environment better than someone who has no work experience." To paraphrase Harry Truman, these students learn to stand the heat by staying in the kitchen. They learn not only how to prepare food, but also how to do it at a professional pace.

For vocational programs at Hocking and elsewhere, the proof of the pudding is in the placement statistics, and a placement survey for fiscal year 1990 found twenty-two of thirty graduates from the culinary program employed in culinary work. Likewise, the telemarketing teacher tells of former students who are now in charge of telemarketing centers in Colorado and North Dakota. The vocational programs with which many SBEs are associated usually have to submit placement statistics to the state, because teaching marketable skills is generally assumed to be the first objective of these SBEs. What should now be apparent is how much else they can do in addition.

4

Economic Contributions

*I*n addition to their educational advantages, SBEs also provide economic benefits. This chapter describes how they produce revenue or reduce costs for schools, subsidize customers or clients by offering goods or services at less than market prices, and promote economic development of the local community. SBEs also make an indirect economic contribution: practices developed in SBEs may point the way for nonschool business enterprises seeking methods to maximize employee learning in the process of production.

A Cost-Benefit Model for SBE

Before describing some of the economic benefits found in our case studies, it is appropriate to ask under what circumstances schools should engage in productive activities. The general answer is that SBEs should undertake activities that are socially beneficial but that would not be feasible for profit-seeking enterprises.

These activities fall into two main categories. In one category are activities from which the benefit to people other than the students involved exceeds the true cost of production, including students' time. What economists call "pure public

80

goods" belong in this category — for example, the restoration of a historic landmark. The use of a pure public good by one person does not diminish its availability for use by other people. Although many people might appreciate the benefit of having the restoration done even if they never visit the site, their potential willingness to pay could not be captured in the form of user fees. The conventional means of financing such projects is either through donations to a not-for-profit organization or through taxation to support a public agency doing the work. A school enterprise is, in fact, a public agency, and the expenditure of resources necessary to produce the public good is justified if the benefit to citizens exceeds the project's cost. The same can be said of activities such as energy conservation and environmental enhancement, which may not be pure public goods but do yield positive spillover benefits to people other than the actual customers or clients. For example, installing energy-efficient lighting not only reduces electricity bills for the property owner but also reduces the environmental damage caused by production of electricity.

In the second category are labor intensive services for which the benefit to customers or clients does not exceed the cost of production but that are of sufficient educational value to participating students that the sum of the educational benefit and the benefit to consumers exceeds production cost. Examples include caring for small children, restoring dilapidated houses or cars, and providing low-volume retail or food services. A profit-seeking enterprise would not be able to break even on such activities, but the SBE would be justified in undertaking them because of the educational benefit to the students involved.

The logic of these calculations becomes clearer if we use some explicit symbols. Let B stand for the benefit from a proposed activity to people other than the students involved. Let S denote the benefit to participating students and C denote the true cost of production, including students' time. B, C, and S are all measured per unit of product or service. Suppose M is the price that could be charged in a competitive market. If $M > C$, the activity could be performed by a profit-seeking business and should not be conducted by a school enterprise. In the

United States, an activity would be considered appropriate for SBE if and only if $S + B > C > M$. In the first category of activities — public goods or activities with positive spillover benefits — it may often be true that $B > C$, so that the project is justified apart from its educational benefit, but $C > M$, because an ordinary business enterprise relying on user fees could not capture all of the benefits. In the second category — labor-intensive services — $B < C$ but $S + B > C > M$.

In practice, it is not usually possible to measure these quantities with any precision, of course. However, these principles provide general guidance in analyzing existing or potential SBEs.

Cost Recovery

By using revenues from the sale of students' work to pay some of the costs of the instructional program, a school may be able to provide some educational services that otherwise might not be offered. As we mentioned in Chapter One, this is one of the oldest and most widespread rationales for school-based enterprise. And in some programs — for example, food preparation — it would be wasteful not to sell what the students produce. The director of the culinary program at Hocking College comments, "If we didn't have an outlet for the volume of food that we purchase, our costs would be significantly greater than what they are. I can't imagine running a production-oriented culinary program and not having a food outlet."

It is not uncommon for SBE revenues to exceed the cost of materials and other operating costs, excluding personnel. The instructor at the Fairfax County car dealership asserts, "After everything was paid last year, they were quite a bit in the black. This year is going to be the same way. We started out in the red, because of our insurance and everything, and by midyear we had already gone in the black, and we're back in the black now. So we're ahead of the game." At the end of the previous year, this program returned $16,000 to the Fairfax Foundation for Applied Technical/Vocational Education.

The cosmetology program at Warren Tech, serving mainly

senior citizens, grossed $90,000 in one year. This covered all costs except the teacher and the facility, in addition to providing funds for other Warren Tech programs.

In some situations, the rules or understandings governing school-based enterprise require any profits to be invested back in the enterprise itself. This is the case at Rothsay, where profits from the store and lumberyard have been used to expand the value of inventory to $44,000 (from the original $30,000). According to the administrator in charge, enterprise profits will also be used to reimburse the school for the cost of a truck that was bought with school funds to be used by the enterprise.

Typically, instructors' salaries are paid by the school and are not expected to be covered by SBE revenues. However, if the SBE is sufficiently profitable, it may find itself paying teachers' salaries too. This appears to have happened in the culinary program at Metro Tech, where the dining room serves approximately 15,000 meals each year and the coffee shop serves forty or fifty customers per day. The present chef, who joined the program six years ago, says that the program made a profit of $40,000 in his first year. Since then, the cost of two salaries has been charged against the program each year.

The child-care center in Brooks County, Georgia, also produces enough revenue to pay the salaries of four teaching aides and the program director, in addition to other expenses. Only one teacher's salary and the building and utilities costs have to be paid by the school.

Revenues from the telemarketing center at Hocking College do not completely cover costs, so the college has to make up the difference. However, the center also provides services to other parts of the college. The center director offers some examples:

> We have, for instance, the National Park Ranger Training Institute. We do all of their calls to try and recruit students. We charge them $.90 a call when they should be charged $3.00 per call. But the president [of the college] basically doesn't want you charging the departments what an outside client would have to pay.

You know what we do for admissions? Five days after the quarter begins, we get a printout of students who didn't return—those enrolled in winter quarter who didn't come back in the spring. We get on the phone, call, and ask where they are. "Well, I ran out of money." "Well, money's not a problem at Hocking College." I mean, you'd be surprised at how many people we've been able to bring back into the fold.

The value of these free or low-priced services to the college may equal or exceed the net cost to the college of operating the center.

In a similar fashion, the hospitality program at Hocking provides space and services that enable the college to sponsor functions at a substantially reduced cost. The director explains:

For instance, we have a large community dinner tonight [for approximately 500 people]. We'll be using all the space that's considered to be classroom space and all the space that's considered to be meeting space. I personally think it's a sin that any academic building at any point in time should have large amounts of vacant space. What we've done over there is schedule classes so that we can have the space available for banquets, special events, functions, and those kinds of things. Having that extra space there has also allowed us to do a number of trade shows related to hospitality. We've had equipment shown over there, and we had the state Department of Travel and Tourism training sessions over there, with representatives from the state of Ohio. The students from all three programs worked together. Travel students serve as hosts and hostesses; the hotel students are the servers; the culinary students prepare the food.

At Hocking, students are usually paid for their work in SBEs. In fact, supporting students is one of the main reasons administrators at Hocking give for organizing SBEs. At the college level, where students' time is a major cost of schooling (given that if they were not in school, they could be gainfully employed), providing opportunities for students to earn money as part of their education is an important part of cost recovery.

The Hocking telemarketing center pays students minimum wage. In the hotel and restaurant at Hocking, students are ordinarily paid $8.00 per hour, but sometimes more. According to the director, "What we do is give them double and triple value time for hours worked on a holiday. So if you stay here on Thanksgiving, Mother's Day, etc., instead of getting the rate of $8.00 an hour, you get $16.00 or $24.00 per hour for the shift. Plus we advertise special packages for the parents to come here and stay on those holidays. You know, a $25.00 room rate, discount meal, etc. And we try to get the students to get their parents to come here as a way to develop a better relationship." This illustrates the entrepreneurial attitude of Hocking College administrators as well as the substantial earning potential for students in Hocking's SBEs.

In addition to working in SBEs or at other campus jobs, Hocking students can earn money working in small businesses operated by the college but not directly tied to the instructional program. The staff member in charge describes some of the activity:

> We're out there to make a profit, and it provides a source of income for some students who have no other source of income. You get a lot of students who come in here and will not qualify for work-study [need-based financial aid], but I can hire them for different businesses we have. For example, in electronics [an electronic equipment repair service] we have electronics students; in Beaver Industries they're natural resource students. We design and manufacture T-shirts for a business called Hocking Special-T's. We use business students for that, and they actually do the work and go out and do the sales and promotion, visiting schools, etc. We

have a room above a local bank, second floor, so
it's not like a storefront for sales; it's that you come
to me and we make some for you.

Some other SBEs also pay students directly. In the Fairfax County Classroom on the Mall, students who work late af-
ternoons, evenings, or weekends are paid; and students in several
other of the enterprises also receive payment when they work
hours other than those normally required in the school day. But
in the construction enterprise at Coop Tech, students are paid
for the hours they work even though they are all during the regular school day.

Although most of our sixteen SBEs do not pay students
wages, they often award other material benefits. In Fairfax
County, the supporting foundation uses some of the revenue
from its various enterprises to give postsecondary scholarships
to several students a year. SBE students in Fairfax and elsewhere are also the beneficiaries of shared income through the
funding of student organizations and of student participation
in state and national conferences and conventions. The computer-aided drafting class at Metro Tech received a $45,000 pur-
chase order from a local aerospace equipment manufacturer to
copy manual drawings onto the computer; proceeds went to the
drafting students' activity fund. And SBEs often use some of
their revenues for special banquets, field trips, and year-end
celebrations.

Southington's school store illustrates the range of purposes
to which SBE profits can be applied. From annual gross sales
of approximately $50,000, the store clears a profit of about
$15,000. A large share of this goes to support DECA activities
for students, including travel to state and national conventions.
Some of the remaining money is donated to charitable causes
in the community, a portion pays expenses for projects of individual students who work in the store, and some is given to other
student clubs on campus.

But *all* SBEs exist for educational purposes, not primarily to make money. As we have explained, SBEs in the United
States normally do not conduct activities in which it would be

possible to cover all production costs at a competitive market price. Though not sufficient to make a commercial profit, the revenue from sale of students' work does help sustain educational programs.

Providing Goods or Services
at Less Than Market Price

In addition to offsetting some costs of the educational program, an SBE also provides an economic benefit to clients or customers if products or services are sold at less than market price. The restriction of SBEs to activities where the cost of production exceeds the competitive market price means that an SBE is not commercially profitable even if students' work is sold at the market price. Nevertheless, some SBEs charge even less than the market price.

Sometimes they can do this because students are paid by a source other than the school or the client. The construction program at Coop Tech in New York City, for example, requires clients to furnish only the building materials. Students' stipends are paid by a government training program, so clients are spared the cost of labor. As a result, the Coop Tech crews are in great demand.

Other New York City schools are especially eager for their services, but the Coop Tech principal says that there are problems working for other schools:

> The thing that we're trying to get away from, because of the red tape and all the bother, is the schools. Because you have problems with the [subdistrict] superintendents. They fight. I work for the alternative school superintendent. When I was doing work for the Manhattan superintendent and not for an alternative school, he got ticked off at me because we were doing work for a Manhattan superintendent. So now I'm doing some work for the alternative school superintendent. Then the Queens superintendent found out what we did in Manhattan.

Now he's got a project for me to do in Queens. So
there are problems, and most of them are political, turf problems, which I don't want to deal with.
It's a lot of headaches. It really is. It's not worth
it. It really isn't.

Problems also arise with other clients — for example, Catholic
Charities:

We worked there for six years with them, all right?
We did seven buildings for them, all right? In six
years. So they got their money's worth out of us.
But on the other hand, we had a lot of problems
with them. Now there are materials sitting down
there that they're going to throw away. Construction materials, plumbing materials, electrical materials, that we could use in this school. So I'm telling them, "If you want me to finish the plumbing,
donate that stuff to the school." Otherwise, we're
not going back there. They can go whistle. "And
if you don't like it, go pay your plumbers to do the
work for you — at $65 an hour. Do it." You know?
So I'm going down there to meet with them on
Tuesday night at five o'clock. And I'm telling them
that if they want us to come back to finish it, first
thing they do is wrap that stuff up; I get the truck
down there; it goes in the truck; and when it's in
the school and off the truck, we'll be there the next
day. Otherwise, no go.

The toughness of this bargaining position is a measure
of how valuable Coop Tech's service is to its clients. However, while providing free student labor benefits clients, it also
potentially threatens private contractors and other school employees, who might otherwise be hired to do the work. (The
problem of where to set prices so as to balance the interests of
consumers and competing suppliers is discussed in Chapter Six.)
Thomas Jefferson High School's mentorship students also
provide free services, and they are not paid from another source.

Mentorship students' work has two kinds of value. First, some of it results in new scientific knowledge. As we noted, students have published papers in engineering and medical-research journals, and the school publishes students' work in its own research journal. Second, as unpaid interns, students contribute their budding expertise to private and public research projects in surrounding labs. The mentorship coordinator offers two examples of mentorship arrangements:

> We have one [student] at the agricultural research center at Beltsville, which is about a forty-five-minute drive from here. She chose to do that. I didn't push her to go there, but she's interested in plant sciences, and there's a place there that's doing research. No other place can equal that. She's working with a mentor who is known in his field and has done a lot of publishing.
>
> We have one at the Bureau of Standards over at Gaithersburg, and that's another forty-five-minute drive. The student again chose that, because he had known about some guy there who was doing research in dentistry. They were doing a study of ceramics, a new material for fillings. So the student is testing the hardness of the ceramics and trying to get the hardness to match the hardness of a tooth.

The labs, and the labs' clients, evidently benefit from the free student interns. However, again the issue arises whether students might be displacing potential *paid* employees.

Community Economic Development

Beyond cost recovery for schools and subsidies for clients or customers, SBEs can also provide various economic benefits to their local communities. These range from stimulating capital accumulation and catalyzing new business ventures in the private sector to providing previously unavailable goods or services to local consumers.

In New York City, Coop Tech's construction project salvages housing that would otherwise remain uninhabitable. This contributes directly to the local capital stock. It also produces positive spillovers, since rehabilitating one structure increases the value of neighboring properties. Furthermore, after students leave the program, they will continue to maintain the local housing stock, not only if they find paid jobs in the construction industry but also if they fix up their own residences and neighborhoods. One student remarks, "You could be your own handyman. If you have an electrical problem, you could fix it up prim and proper. You could install new tile. This is a good advantage, to me. One time a teacher in this program told me how he built his own house because he knows how to do everything, with the foundation, built the house, everything. And that's good. So someday I can do that."

A teacher at Belle Fourche describes how he and his students spearheaded a plan to restore one of the town's historic buildings:

> It's an old poolhall. Early on it was a whorehouse. It has a lot of Old West history attached. It has about $10,000 in taxes against it. The county was really interested in selling it. No one wanted to buy it. A few students and I and a few others wanted to preserve it. We approached the county commissioners and we said, "We aren't interested in the business of ownership of that particular facility, but could we, as an educational project and also one that has entrepreneurial overtones, take this on? The Historical Society — if you would deed it over to them, or lease it, then we would lease it from them for $1 a year. The school attorney says we can do that."
>
> So we had this building. It's about 35 to 40 feet wide, made out of sandstone, three stories high, and about 100-something feet long. It's leaking, and it's dirty, and it's dumpy.
>
> So one class went down; they put it on a

CAD system they've known about. They've done all the measurements and this and that, and we had the artist bunch; they did the artist's rendition. They got hold of one of the historic preservation experts from Deadwood, and he told them this window is authentic, this one isn't, etc. So the kids drew in the authentic ones, and now we have a rendition of what it would look like. Now I think we'll get that building, and I'm proud that we'll get that thing restored.

SBEs can also contribute to community economic development by providing goods or services that would otherwise be unavailable. Opportunities to do this are greatest in small, remote communities. One of the students at Belle Fourche has started his own printing business, for example, and it is helping to keep the local printers up-to-date:

I invested in a $4,000 computer and laser printer. I have basically the same capabilities as the best printer in town. I have the same capabilities as he does, and I just do printing for different people. I've done graduation announcements for the school here. Just a little bit of everything. I've got a large market now. There are a lot of people who think, "Just a kid — he can't do good work." Actually, I've got quite a few good customers. As a matter of fact, one of the printing businesses here in town — his equipment was getting really old, and he didn't have much for equipment. Now I'm contracted out with him. Everything he does goes through me. I do all the setup and stuff for him.

By reopening the town's only hardware and lumber dealer, the Rothsay SBE is maintaining an important source of supplies for the local community. As one student observes, "One of the things that the community definitely gets out of it is a hardware store. It's a service. One nice thing with the grocery store [a project in the planning stage] is that a lot of our town is elderly people who aren't able to go out on their own, or don't like to travel to Fergus or Barnesville or Pelican to get their groceries or gifts, etc. It's good for the community to have this. It keeps the community together. We have great community support." As the school principal puts it, "If you wanted a box of screws before we reopened the store, you had to drive fifteen miles for a $.98 box."

The superintendent at Mt. Edgecumbe relates how he helped create SBEs to provide unavailable goods and services in the seacoast hamlet of Metlakatla, where he was previously stationed as school superintendent:

> We also opened up a bakery. There was no bakery in the village, so one day a week the people in the town could come to school and buy their baked goods. Then we set up another business. We got a Mercury marine dealership for the school. We sent our vocational education teacher back to Wisconsin, got him trained and certified as a mechanic. Then we started stocking all these Mercury outboards and inboard/outboards and a whole parts inventory and everything else. So we had students involved in inventory and sales. People would come in and try to figure out what they needed. We got the business teacher involved. His class started to do all the spreadsheets, and they also started selling all the baked goods out of that classroom. Then we got the other shop teacher going on boat building, and we started to manufacture aluminum skiffs.

The bakery contributed to improving the quality of local life, and the boat and motor enterprise contributed to helping local residents improve their own productivity and standard of living.

While at Metlakatla, the superintendent started the smoked salmon enterprise that he later brought to Mt. Edgecumbe. He tells how he came to realize that this enterprise was potentially significant not only for the local community but also as an example of what could be done to develop the state of Alaska.

> I was in another meeting and a school board member came up and said, "I need to talk to you about something." He said, "I tasted your fish last year, and that's the best smoked fish I've ever tasted." He said, "I work out of McKinley National Park," which is out of Anchorage, and he said, "We take all these tourists out every day in buses. There are no restaurants in the park, so we have to give them a box lunch. There are twelve different things that we put in that lunch box, and what we'd like is a two-ounce piece of vacuum-packed salmon to go in, because it's made by Alaskan students, it's an Alaskan product, and we think we could get a lot of play out of that." So I said, "How many do you need?" and he said, "Fifty thousand. Can you do it?" And I said, "Well, with that kind of an order, we'll have to get private industry to help us," but I said, "Here's what I can guarantee you: if I get private industry to help us, I'll guarantee you that they'll use our recipe and our labels and everything else, and we'll just contract the service out to them but it'll be our product." He said, "That's fair enough." So I went to Ketchikan and made an agreement with a place called Silver Lining Seafoods, which is now a big-time operation. We did 2,000 of them, and they did 48,000. And so that started it. The next summer, I was contacted by the riverboat people, who said all these people are coming on the boats raving about this fish that they got in their box, and they want it on the boat. We need 50,000 packages. So we go back to our supplier, and he set that one up too. So he ended up with a huge order.

In this true-life fish story, an SBE acted as a catalyst for regional economic development, drawing in tourist dollars, expanding the market for Alaskan products, and creating business for a local manufacturer.

Since coming to Mt. Edgecumbe, the superintendent has continued to use school-based enterprise as a catalyst. For example, the smoked fish recipe has been shared with a local business.

> We've turned over our recipe to a local business here who asked us for it. I think they've got something like $300,000 or $400,000 into this new business. We're trying to help. We think that we ought to partner with business. We feel that business gives education a lot, and education ought to give something back.
>
> In one instance, this guy was in his office getting things set up and a Korean importer walks in and says, "I'm looking for salmon products. Do you have any samples? I understand that you're starting a new business." "Yes, I do. I've got some in the back room." Well, he goes in the back room. The only samples he's got are ours. So he gives this Korean our product, and the Korean says, "That's exactly what I want. And I need . . . "—I can't remember what he said, somewhere in the neighborhood of $250,000 or something of this product within four months or something. Well, there's no way you're going to be able to do that. I mean, doing salmon is a year cycle. You have to know ahead of time how much fish you're going to need and all those kinds of things. Anyway, he ended up selling to Japanese rather than Korean. He didn't go with the initial order that this guy made. But it just pointed out that that lox product was a product that Asians liked. He told me he just finished an order to Japan about two weeks ago. So they're coming on our coattails, so to speak.

Mt. Edgecumbe has now formalized this kind of relationship with local business by advertising in the Sitka newspaper for partners who want the SBE to help with new-product development. The enterprise teacher explains this step:

> The class put out a request for proposals for the class to assist the processor in developing new ideas, new directions, new products. Our group had two proposals, and they chose Sitka Sound Seafoods. What we're doing for them right now is trying to develop a new product line. They're interested in going into gift package and retail outlet sales here in Sitka as well as through mail order. Our group is working to develop a kipper strip, a small sample size that they can put into their gift packages. And we're using different types of fish. The class is trying different types of fish that Sitka Sound Seafoods provided, and we're keeping information in our logs and own notes as to what happens to each product that we use. So far we haven't had any luck with what Sitka Sound Seafoods has provided us. They've provided us with steelhead and king. For our product we use sockeye, which is easy to work with, and it's been very successful. So we're trying to work with Sitka Sound Seafoods, but they need to come up with a way to handle the fish, presenting it to us so we can process it.

From this kind of partnership, the commercial fish processor may obtain valuable information about potential new products and how to produce and market them.

In addition to developing the regional economic base, this partnership is also preparing students who will contribute to future economic development. The Mt. Edgecumbe superintendent is determined to equip students to transform Alaska's economy: "You see, we're the fourteenth colony, Alaska. What we do is ship out all of our raw product and then buy it back in a finished form. We've somehow got to change that. I'm on a vendetta to get that changed. In twenty years, these kids will be running the import-export business in Alaska."

Hocking College also plays a deliberate part in state economic development. Like other states, Ohio uses its two-year technical colleges as technology transfer agents. The telemarketing director at Hocking serves as the campus coordinator for OTTO, the Ohio Technology Transfer Organization. He describes the concept of OTTO and tells how he created the telemarketing facility to help local business:

> There's a lot of research being conducted in major institutions, federal laboratories, and smaller institutions. A lot of times, this R&D never gets plugged into business and industry in a particular state. We go out and call up small business and industry. We go to a business, and they say they're having a little difficulty forming this metal piece. We have access to federal laboratories, we have access to major colleges and universities, we have data bases, so we hope to be able to provide some appropriate technology to these businesses and industries. We deal with computer problems to engineering problems, to sophisticated materials problems, to marketing problems — virtually any kind of technology-based problem.
>
> I was working with a company here in town that manufactures outdoor footware. They're one of the largest in the U.S. that still manufactures outdoor footware. It's the William Brooks shoe company, but they're under a trade name called Rocky Boots. I've known the Brooks family. I've been here for twenty-two years. In 1985 I did a little dog and pony show for business and industry called "marketing action plans," where we try to list the strengths of the company and then we try to build some new marketing opportunities around what they believe their strengths have been. The first four or five items on the list had to do with wanting to use more 1-800 kinds of service. They wanted to get closer to the ultimate customer who would be purchasing and using the footware, and they wanted to get

closer to retailers. They wanted to be able to provide much better information and a link between
the retailers and the ultimate consumers.

I saw all this, and I didn't know too much
about telemarketing at the time — probably as much
as you. I thought it was those people who called
you during your dinner hour. So I did some research myself, and the more I found out about
telemarketing, the more I found it could be a viable opportunity as a curriculum, because at the time
there was no curriculum in telemarketing throughout the country; and I thought since *profit*'s not a
dirty word here at the college, we could develop
a telemarketing center using a couple of anchor
clients or key clients. That could subsidize some
of the training we do, but we could make it a cost-
effective way for these businesses to plug into our
college and get some value-added service that doesn't
cost an arm and a leg. I went to Mike Brooks and
his VP for sales and marketing, took them to lunch
and told them I had an idea that might sound a
little farfetched, but I didn't get more than ten words
out of my mouth when Mike Brooks said, "Let's
do it. We're a major player; we want to be part of
this." So we developed a telemarketing center. They
brought us subsequent clients.

We've been very successful with the program
too. In 1988 we won the prestigious Tele-Award
from the American Telemarketing Association.
We're the only college in the country that offers
telemarketing as an A.A. degree but also has a for-
profit telemarketing center.

The telemarketing program contributes to regional economic development in other ways as well. One student, disabled by the disease lupus, will be able to earn a living at
home as a telemarketing subcontractor; a former student is
able to stay home with her children and earn money telemarket-

ing. These examples suggest that telemarketing can provide employment (or self-employment, in the case of subcontractors) for individuals who otherwise would not be gainfully employed. The center director envisions that telemarketing will create employment opportunities on a substantial scale:

> I think telemarketing really fits in the economic development picture in rural communities, and I'll tell you why. If you go through Nelsonville and you look up at the second, third, fourth floor of some of these buildings — they're empty. My vision is to get those second, third, fourth floors filled with really nice, clean, wholesome, good-environment [telemarketing] centers. And then, Mr. Landlord, go and put signs in front of your building: office space or retail space available. Instead of $1,200 or $1,500 a month, $300 a month, because you've already helped amortize the second, third, and fourth floor. The retail businesses will come in and stay there. They'll have a captive audience, because you've got employees on the second and third floor.

The telemarketing SBE thus becomes a model for community economic development.

SBE as a Model Workplace

The most far-reaching, but still most unrealized, potential economic benefit from SBE is its ability to pioneer in methods of production that maximize learning. As accelerating changes in technology and markets require ever-faster adaptation, large and small companies in the United States and abroad struggle to become learning organizations. Giving employees more instruction off the job is only part of the solution. Continuous improvement in quality and efficiency under changing conditions also requires employers somehow to engineer more learning into the work process itself. Methods for doing this are still largely unknown.

SBEs are ideal laboratories for experimenting with techniques to incorporate learning into production. Education is their primary mission; they use productive activity to accomplish it. But few SBEs have experimented in any systematic or self-conscious way with how to organize productive activity so as to maximize learning.

Among our sixteen cases, Mt. Edgecumbe has gone farthest in this direction, due to its schoolwide emphasis on formal procedures for continuous improvement. The evolution of Edgecumbe Enterprises into a fairly routine fish-processing operation cum innovative product-development laboratory is therefore instructive. It may suggest that maximum learning occurs when production workers are also involved with research and development. This idea, which goes beyond the increasingly common corporate practice of engaging front-line workers in process innovation through "quality circles" or "total quality management," suggests the direction in which employment practices are heading. At the highly innovative Saturn automobile manufacturing company, for example, production workers and the United Auto Workers union have been involved since the start of the business in helping to design Saturn cars and the technology to produce them. Because Mt. Edgecumbe students and faculty are at the forefront of contemporary practice, they are frequently invited to speak at meetings of corporate managers dealing with total quality management.

The director of the hospitality program at Hocking College cites another example of potential SBE leadership: the possible introduction of skill-based pay, or pay for knowledge, in Hocking's hotel enterprise. This compensation practice, which has been adopted by a number of U.S. manufacturers and some employers in service industries (U.S. Department of Labor, 1988), rewards employees for what they have shown they know and can do, not just for the job assignments they hold during the pay period. Skill-based pay clearly gives employees an incentive to learn. However, according to the Hocking administrator, it has not been applied in the hospitality industry:

> The hotel industry has had the luxury of an excess
> labor pool, and they haven't been forced into that.
> The assumption is that you can pay any dumbo to
> do anything in a hotel, and therefore employee
> turnover is an accepted part of the business. But
> if the labor shortage becomes more credible, I think
> it will have a lot more merit. I would design it so
> that you get paid for each cross-trained skill you
> learn, and when you get to level 5, you become an
> assistant manager.

It remains to be seen whether Hocking will try out skill-based pay in its hotel. But this kind of pioneering is clearly within the realm of possibility.

Another Hocking College administrator relates how his service as a provider of training to a local company improved the firm's human resource management practice.

> We work with a company called PPC Airfoils. I
> wrote the [training] proposal for that company. We
> used the [SBE] concept with them in reverse. We
> put into place a training program, but their train-
> ing program moved to another building. The build-
> ing included a site which was like the site on the
> [production] floor. So what happened was this: the
> last three weeks of the training, the people pro-
> duced, and their efficiency rating was much higher
> than people on the floor.

If school-based enterprise is an example of learning by doing, this use of firm-based training for actual production could be called doing by learning. It is a concept that a growing number of learning-intensive companies are beginning to recognize (Stern, 1992a).

Some SBEs are developing innovative management processes without (yet) any explicit intention of providing a model for private industry. For example, the experimental team incentive structure at the Fairfax Classroom on the Mall (described

further in Chapter Seven) might offer useful lessons to commercial retailers, though for now the SBE teachers are thinking only
about how their own enterprise could operate more effectively.
Even without taking a self-conscious leadership role, every SBE
must find a way to blend education with production, making
sure that the pressure to get work done does not displace attention from what students are intended to learn. (Further discussion of this balancing act is also included in Chapter Seven.)

The development of more efficient methods to combine
learning with production is an example of creating pure public
goods, because once these methods become known, they are
available to anyone. SBEs are particularly appropriate institutions to develop these methods, not only because using production to promote education is their primary purpose but also because they have more incentive than a nonschool enterprise to
give the information away. A profit-seeking business can derive a competitive advantage from discovering new ways to
stimulate employees' curiosity and channel it into continuous
improvement of products and processes. It is in the interest of
such a company to prevent competitors from copying its successful practices. In contrast, the SBE exists to educate students
by producing benefits for the public at large. One of the most
significant public benefits is the invention of techniques to increase what students learn through production of goods and
services.

5

Social Benefits

Chapter Three described a range of learning outcomes from school-based enterprise. These benefit students by increasing their future income or quality of life. The economic benefits outlined in Chapter Four accrue to schools, SBE customers, local communities, or society at large. In this chapter, we describe nonmaterial outcomes from school-based enterprise that benefit society at large. These include a heightened concern among students for the quality of goods or services they are producing, an increased interest among students in community service, and a reduced risk of dropping out of high school.

Concern for Quality

Craftsmanship is an old-fashioned word for knowing how to do a job right and caring enough to do it that way. The concept of craftsmanship applies not only to the production of tangible goods but also to the provision of services; it pertains to computer programming and retail selling just as it does to construction or car repair. When craftsmanship — or, in gender-neutral form, a craftworker mentality — is present, buyers can be confident of getting their money's worth. Though the price may not be low, buyers can feel that they are getting good value. Because craftsmanship yields more of what economists call "consumers' surplus," it tends to be in short supply. Increasing the number of people who approach their work with a combination of caring and know-how will increase the general level of satisfaction and well-being in society at large.

Although the quality mentality reveals itself in deeds more than words, it can be verbalized, as in these words from a student involved with the experimental aquaculture project in Marion County: "We're taking care of everything. If we have problems, we have to make decisions. In aquaculture, our advisers don't make decisions for us. Everything we do there is hands-on, and we're the ones doing it. If we mess up, we have to work a little bit harder to make changes, to make it a little bit better."

SBEs can encourage development of a craftworker mentality, but some do so more than others. Students' concern for quality depends largely on teachers' insistence on it. It also depends both on the extent to which the quality of what is produced can be attributed to individuals and on the consequences of poor quality: a botched brake repair or faulty electrical wiring is much more serious than a poorly seasoned soup. Regulations, codes, and licensing laws help enforce standards in SBEs in which health or safety demands quality—for example, child-care facilities, food service, and construction. Whether an SBE can be selective in recruiting and retaining students also affects its ability to achieve high standards of quality.

The teacher who directs the Fairfax County car-repair enterprise insists on high quality. A student comments that this teacher "pretty much makes sure that all the cars are in tip-top shape after we're done. He'll check every car. If it isn't done right, he won't let it leave." As a result, students themselves learn not to tolerate defective work. One student crew leader affirms, "If they [his crew] are doing something wrong, it will come back to you. We really try to keep other people out of trouble. If something is messed up on it, if something is not right, if somebody does something wrong, we should tell."

A teacher in the housing rehabilitation enterprise at Coop Tech explains how he reinforces students' awareness of quality:

You insist on it. If it's not done that way, they have
to redo it. The biggest problem for them to understand is what quality is. A lot of them seem to feel
that if it's done, it's done. That's it. It's good enough.
If you put something up and it stays together, it
doesn't collapse, it's okay. Because they really don't
know. The second time around they'll know better, because they had to do it. It's like the beams—if
they're not level, they have to be jacked up and re-
done. That's the rule. I mean, it has to be that way.
This is the key, I mean you just keep reinforcing,
saying it has to be that way. This is industry standards. It's the way it's got to be done.

In a similar vein, a teacher at Belle Fourche remarks,
"Time is money, but so is good workmanship. [A student may
say,] 'I don't have time to do it.' If you don't have time to do
it right, then you're going to have to have time to do it over!
That's kind of the way it goes. We've had to do a lot over. Big
hurry, slap-it-up job. So pride is involved."

Pride is evident in this statement by the chef at Metro
Tech about what he tries to teach his students. "I want the food
to be—as well as looking really nice—I want it to be nutritious,
and I want it to be healthful. And so the sauces—I don't use
any kind of *roux* [thickener made from flour and butter] in my
sauces. Everything is natural. Usually it's a reduction sauce,
like the crawfish sauce we have with mushrooms. I want the
customer to enjoy the bouquet, flavor of the crawfish. But I don't
want it overpowering. So that's what I'm trying to bring to these
kids."

Not all teachers are so scrupulous, however. At a marketing enterprise where profits were given a high priority, the instructor modeled unethical selling by pretending to customers
that he was almost out of a particular product and that they
had better buy it before it was gone. While reflecting the reality of many businesses, this is not a lesson that schools should
be teaching.

Maintaining high standards in SBEs depends not only on

teachers' insistence on quality but also on whether students' actions have important consequences, as we noted. The principal at Rothsay explains how the real consequences of faulty accounting require attention to accuracy:

> We require, locally, that they have a computer class and at least accounting I, and generally speaking all the kids that [the SBE teacher] has also have taken accounting II. Now, the work's got to be accurate, because that data is run through Region I and it's audited. So they're doing the real thing. There can't be any mistakes in it. In a business simulation, if they get it wrong, Randy can go through it and say, "You made some mistakes here, but it isn't going to screw up the business." This could. So they're accountable.

One of the Rothsay students affirms that accountability is taken seriously: "If we make a mistake, if we send a bill to somebody and it's $5 off, they'll come to us and we'll have to tell them what we did, how we set it up, and we'll have to fix it ourselves. It's real stuff. You have to write them a letter and tell them you're sorry and explain what you did."

A student at the Fairfax County Classroom on the Mall believes that the existence of the whole program depends on students' doing things right: "You aren't going to learn anything if it doesn't run right. If it doesn't work, they'll have to close the store down, and we will have lost one of the main employment spots."

At Hocking College, the notion that students' work should have real consequences was part of the institution's founding philosophy. One of the top administrators makes a key distinction:

> A practice experience isn't a hands-on experience. Hands-on teaching experience means that you do the job; you face the consequences. A practice experience is you do the job, you evaluate as to whether I think you can do it. So if you really be-

lieve that you're a technical institute, the whole concept of enterprise has to be a part of the system.
That's if you want the real hands-on uniqueness.
Anybody, anywhere, at any time can create a *practice* experience. You don't need a new college to do
that. A university could do it. The high school could
do it. The county human services training program
could do it. No problem. So why build new walls?
Why spend new dollars if all you're doing is re-creat-
ing in another setting the same thing that anybody
could have done anyway? And heaven forbid, why
hire another 300 staff members? Now, I know that's
a far-out look at it, but in reality it's the whole concept. I think this is where John [the college's founding president] was coming from. He was a tool- and
die-maker.

However, not all SBEs emphasize the consequences of
student behavior. For example, some programs wage a constant
but halfhearted battle against petty theft. In one school-run restaurant, the jar where customers leave tips has been stolen
several times. At one school store, students tend to take candy
bars, literally eating up their own profits. The teacher cannot
watch every candy bar and every mouth all the time, and students do not prevent others from stealing. On the other hand,
students at another school store said stealing was not a problem. "We haven't come across that yet. Everybody really works
hard. Nobody wants to goof up or take a candy bar and not
pay for it."

An SBE's success in maintaining high standards depends
on how effectively teachers communicate those standards, on
the seriousness of consequences, on students' sense that they own
the program, and on the attitudes students bring with them.
At the time they join a school enterprise, students vary widely
in their concern for quality. Some are already meticulous—
among them, a few of the students in a cabinet-making program, whose teacher reports, "The first thing they do is wash
their hands when they go to work. Those are my best cabinet

makers: fussy, just like a surgeon!" However, most students do not arrive with such high standards. The culinary teacher at Metro Tech is frustrated by students who do not even show up — the first necessary ingredient of quality work. Because his program operates on a different schedule than other programs, students cannot get there on the regular school bus, "so we rely on them getting here on their own. And if they show up, well, then we're in good shape. But there are days when none of them show up and then you've got banquets, you've got the coffee shop going, you've got the gourmet room going, and then the staff has to do everything. I mean, you have some that are just excellent, and they're here every day. But there was one student I had — for some reason, he's out all this week. And he's a good kid. But you just never know."

The development of concern for quality can become a major objective of an SBE. One student in the Fairfax car-repair business describes how his attitude improved. "I used to think, well, it's not my car. What you have to do is pretend that every car is yours. Last year I didn't feel like working on them sometimes. The instructor was like, 'What if it was your car?' So every car I do as if it were my own car. I make sure I get it right the first time. If not, then it might not be right, and I'll tear it apart again."

The result of this insistence on quality in the car dealership is a good reputation in the community. The teacher proudly points out how much he and his students are trusted by customers. "You look there. There's maybe a $30,000 to $40,000 engine, a T-Bird engine over there. The car is worth that much, and the community has entrusted us to restore it, repaint it, even to rebuild it. I've got a kid that's a junior in high school who's putting that motor together, trusted with $3,000 or $4,000 worth of parts."

Some SBE students work in similar jobs outside of school and are therefore in a position to compare modes of operation. One of the Fairfax car-dealership students remarks that the SBE does not perform work the customers have not requested, unlike an outside service station, where "they try to push more sales, more than what [the car] came in for." Another student corroborates: "Here I think it's better, because some stores might just try to get you for your money. Here we're not really getting paid for it. We're trying to learn. In some gas stations, they cheat some stuff. In here we really can't." Another example comes from the auto-body shop at Warren Tech, where a student complains that, in the nonschool shop where he works on weekends, the employer often okays what the student considers shoddy work to save labor time.

A student in the Brooks County child-care program suggests that the SBE's commitment to quality is comparable to another licensed day-care center where she works: "I've worked a whole day [at the other center], just me and eight of them. We [at school] work just as hard to see that the quality is there. We're working with children and babies, and it has to be done right all the time." But a student at the Metro Tech child-care center in Phoenix, asked if she had liked working after school at a private day-care center, replies, "No, it was dirty and they didn't follow the rules they were supposed to. They had five-year-olds with one-year-olds mixed up in the same room. It just didn't look like it was safe for kids to be there."

Quality in SBEs may be as good or better than in outside work—but that is not always the case. The Gateway Tech radio station demonstrates the difficulty sometimes encountered in trying to maintain a professional level of quality. The teacher concedes that students

> get a little sloppy when it's only an assignment, and I'm the only one that hears it. But when it's going to be used on the air, like if a student does a commercial for someone that he sold, you can hear how much more they put into it because it's their pride and joy going on the air. The competition and the adrenaline of being at a real station; you can't duplicate that in this kind of setting [which broadcasts only by cable circuit]. They always know it's not real here. But if they go over and suddenly get a part-time job at JZQ, they'll sound and do things there in a more professional way. . . .
>
> The rule on indecency is you're not supposed

to be able to broadcast indecency before 8 P.M. The safe harbor is 8 P.M. to 6 A.M. Obscenity, you can't broadcast that any time. I've pulled some students off [of air time] for half a semester for using the *F* word.

A student in the Gateway program describes the kind of irresponsible behavior that sometimes occurs: "People go around bumping each other's carts [containing tapes for broadcast]. For a semester and a half it went like that. People were bumping each other's carts for fun. After you spend an hour or two making those tapes, they go in there and ruin it. Yesterday we put our cart in there and played it, and all you hear is *whoop whoop whoop*. It was gone."

At the other end of the spectrum are examples of SBE students taking extraordinary responsibility. The Rothsay SBE teacher marvels, "When we first started in [the store], I had ten kids that were busters. I mean these kids worked hard. In this snowstorm — there wasn't school that day — I had kids down there at ten minutes to eight in the morning to open the store. They painted on their free time. I had four boys that cleaned the yard out. Fire inspector said, 'You got to get that forty years of [saw]dust out of there.' Those kids really worked hard."

In the Fairfax County Classroom on the Mall, students acting as supervisors are forced to deal with the range of motivation among their peers. A student manager tells us,

> Another problem is that for a lot of people who work at the Marketplace, it's the first job they've ever had, and they don't know what it's like in a job. A lot of people don't take it seriously. Not people in this [marketing] program, but people outside the program that work [for pay in the kiosk]. They don't seem to take it as seriously as we do. And you just have to let them know they're going to take it seriously or they're not going to work there. There's no adult supervision. They know we're running it, and they think they can get away with a lot. We're right around their age, so we'll let them get away

with it — that's what they think. They treat it like
class — some people do — but there are some that are
real responsible and work really hard.

To enforce high standards of service, teachers send "secret
shoppers" to make observations in the Classroom on the Mall:

We just ask some of the local merchants. That's part
of [the students'] team score. They don't know when
a secret shopper is coming. So that, hopefully, keeps
a high level of customer service all the time. We
just go and ask a merchant if he'll go by the store
and write down what he observed. It's very informal. But it's enough that we come back the next
day and say, 'It was observed that you were eating
at the Marketplace when you should have been doing something else.' That's enough to let them know
that somebody is watching. We try to make sure
that every team has at least one secret shopper visit.
That secret shopper fills out an evaluation form,
and that determines their team score.

Teachers who succeed in instilling a dedication to high
standards in students, like successful teachers in any area, must
earn students' trust and respect. In order to get students to care
about the work, teachers must show that they care about students. One of the students in the Fairfax County car dealership
tells how the teacher won him over: "I lost my license in March,
and he would come over to Langley and pick me up every day.
He's real good. He's more than a teacher; he's also a friend.
I deal with him as a friend or a dad. He more or less can be
a second dad in a way, when you really think about it." To which
another student responds, "Better than my dad. At least when
you think of him as a dad, you can walk away from this one.
The other one keeps following you around."
    The same mixture of respect and affection is expressed
by a student in the Coop Tech construction program, who says
of his teacher, "He knows a lot. He's like that big brother."
    The respect students give their SBE teachers comes in part

from regard for the teachers' experience in the industry, which gives legitimacy to their demands. A chef in charge of a school restaurant enterprise has this to say:

> The other problem, though, with these kids is that as an industry, this stuff has to be done every day. And they seem to think, "Well, I've done it two or three times; I know how to do it. I never want to do it again." You know, it's a job that has to be done. I don't always walk around with a smile on my face. I run the kitchen. I'm firm. I don't abuse them or anything. But I demand respect too. And if there's a job to do, I expect them to do it. If we have a problem, then we'll sit down and we'll talk about it. We'll work it out. But I run the program the same way I ran my kitchen when I was in industry. Because I want the student to know what it's really like.

On the other hand, industry standards sometimes fail to contribute to students' respect for themselves or what they are doing. In one of the construction programs, students have been working at the same site for ten years, building houses and taking classes. Just as on a commercial construction site, there are portable toilets only, no running water, and temporary trailers are used for classrooms. Students could have been organized to build more adequate facilities for themselves, but this has never been done. Instead, they continue to feel the indignity of these shoddy conditions and the frustration of not being in a position to ameliorate them. These feelings interfere with their commitment to do high-quality work.

An argument can be made that SBEs should replicate the bad as well as the good aspects of nonschool enterprise, as part of showing students how it really is. On the other hand, the great majority of high school students manage to find nonschool jobs on their own. Some researchers have found that experience in these outside jobs, which are often unchallenging and repetitive, tends to make students cynical about work (Greenberger and Steinberg, 1986; Steinberg, Fegley, and Dornbusch, 1993). Rather than trying to reproduce the negative aspects of work, a more constructive role for SBEs is to demonstrate the positive possibilities. Giving students the experience of good work may help them establish personal standards that will help them know what to look for in the labor market.

Community Service

In addition to learning a craftworker mentality on the job, some SBE students also learn the satisfaction of community service. One student remarks that her work in a school store "gives me a sense of pride and pleasure of doing something right, something for my school, and helping serve the community." At rural enterprises such as those in Rothsay, Belle Fourche, and Mt. Edgecumbe, students are aware that they provide valuable services to their local communities.

Some of the students involved in Southington's school store are using their knowledge of retailing to help set up a store for a health-care center. According to the teacher,

> Bradley Hospital Corporation just built what's called a health-care center, for people who can still get some health services. Our kids are working on setting up a store for them, to sell all of their products on site right at Bradley Memorial Hospital. We have a team of seven or eight kids out there — next year's kids, who are juniors now — they're in the process of setting that up. There will be some volunteer time there. The final goal is to have people who live there run it. The kids are doing a layout and getting merchandise lined up, trying to figure out how they're going to do things. What they're going to do is go over the layout of it and envision what merchandise should be carried there, and they're going to make some decision on whether to set it up.

He explains how he chose one of the students to work on this project, and some of the incentives in addition to pure service: "One of the girls wanted to be an officer [in the DECA club], and she didn't get elected. She's very enthusiastic. I didn't want to lose her from the program, so I asked her if she would be interested in doing some kind of project, because we can then write it up and submit it for competition. I also know that she had a group of girlfriends who were also in my classes, and I figured that they would do it together. She's now sort of like the coordinator."

Of the SBEs we observed, the one with the most explicit emphasis on community service is at the Marion County Technical Center, which participates in the Building Our American Communities contest sponsored by Future Farmers of America. Students have contributed efforts of sufficient impact to win or be a finalist in the national contest year after year. A student describes one of the projects and its enthusiastic reception:

> We took 2,000 marigolds down there, 500 flats—some we raised, some we bought from [another FFA chapter]. We sell to the Chamber of Commerce, and they resell for their fund-raiser. The object is for us to have somebody to give our flowers to. The Chamber of Commerce uses them for the beautification of downtown. The project serves more than one purpose, more than one undertaking.
>
> It was really a good sale. We brought 500 flats, and as fast as we could unload them, they were buying them. They take them right off the truck. In fact, while the truck was backing up, one guy jumped up on the back, trying to take flowers off of it. We got worried about public safety.

Another Marion County student declares his intention to keep doing community work in the tradition of agricultural service: "I'm going to major in ag business or farm management. I feel that anybody being in an ag field, all the agriculture works together in some way. You got the Farm Bureau and different people. The skills we learned here are going to turn right back and relate to our jobs in community development. Somehow we will always be working with people. FFA taught us lots of how to do that."

Student Retention

Teachers and students testify that participation in an SBE helps motivate students to finish high school. In addition to benefiting the would-be dropouts themselves, dropout prevention also benefits society at large, because graduates are less likely to commit crimes and impose other burdens on society.

SBEs keep some students in school by giving them a real context for their schoolwork. One student at Metro Tech says of the SBE restaurant program, "It kept me in school."

The teacher in the Fairfax car dealership comments on how the program keeps students attending school: "Kids told me this morning, 'Well, we don't mind coming to your class; it's the other ones afterwards.' Some kids get up and come to our classes just because they want to do something that day. Sure, they have to go to English and math afterwards, but at least they're up."

At Coop Tech in New York City, students spend one week working on the apartment rebuilding project, then the next week at their home high schools, taking double periods of English, math, and other core subjects. One student indicates that this arrangement helped him stay in school:

> I find it easier, because you're not always in school. It's not that you're in school that much, I just find it easier some way. When tests come up, everybody knows what's going to happen, because they give it to you the same week. I find it much easier to do this than go to school week after week. I never used to like going to school at all. I used to hardly be in school. Most of the time, I used to go and hang out with my friends and cut out of school. But now, since I'm in this program, you know, I be looking forward to coming to work. But then the week that I got to go to school, I'll just be like, "Oh I just got to go through this week, and then next week I'll be working."

The superintendent at Mt. Edgecumbe describes how the SBE program helps some students who do not experience a sense of accomplishment in other activities:

> What we've found in our entrepreneurship program is that the nonathletes, the noncheerleaders, the people who aren't in anything are the kids that really gravitate to that program and really show success, because it's a way that those kids can achieve. It's something they can be proud of. They can come out with a product, and they've never produced anything in their lives. And when they finish a label or they finish a package or they come up with a new idea — I mean, God, they just beam. And it's a lot of our lower-end kids that end up in those kinds of programs and show the greatest success. At-risk students need programs like that. That's exactly what at-risk kids need. Unless they can feel good about themselves, they're not going to be able to be educated.

This perception of the SBE as an alternative arena for achievement is echoed by a teacher in the Fairfax County Classroom on the Mall:

> One of the comments we get a lot from guidance counselors is that sometimes they're surprised that a student who may be a very high performer here is a very poor performer back at the high school. You would have had no idea. It's kind of nice too. I think that sometimes when you have a lot of teachers, and the student is having some difficulties at school, your expectations for that student are lowered. Over here, we don't have those expectations. They all come in here, and we don't know anything about them. We're sometimes shocked when we go and find out that our class is the only one they attend. "So-and-so has been having these problems, cutting classes." It happens all the time.

Along much the same lines, the Southington SBE teacher describes how some students who do not stand out in high school can excel in the school store and related activities:

> When you look at sophomores and juniors who come into this school, who aren't in the top quarter of the class as far as academics are concerned but who have some talents and abilities, who have never really been able to shine before, who now get involved in the marketing ed program and run the store or who get involved in the competitions — every year we send about eight to ten kids to the national [DECA competition] — it's a tremendous opportunity for them, and the kids know that. They work very hard at that. The employer luncheon that they run, and the programs that they run — when you see what those kids have accomplished, in terms of their own self-concept, and particularly in terms of their own self-confidence, I think it's a tremendous program for these kids.

In Brooks County, one potential dropout was kept in school several years ago by a building trades program in which he is now an instructor. His supervisor, who knew him then, describes him as "a kid that possibly would have dropped out of school, probably would not have been as successful as he has been if it hadn't been for that. He now has a teaching license and is certified as a T and I [trades and industry] instructor." In this role, he is in a position to exert a positive influence on the next generation of would-be dropouts.

The principal of the Fairfax County construction program, to which a large proportion of students are assigned because they have had academic or disciplinary problems in their home high school, believes that the program keeps some students (though not all) from dropping out. "You're going to lose three out of ten. Of that seven [who remain], you have five of them that graduate. That's 50 percent more than would have graduated if they hadn't come here."

PART THREE

Creating a
School-Based Enterprise

6

Getting Started

Several issues face those who initiate a school enterprise. These include deciding what goods or services to produce, avoiding competition with local suppliers, setting appropriate prices, hiring qualified staff, and recruiting students. We discuss these issues in this chapter.

Deciding What to Produce

The choice of product or service can make or break the enterprise. If demand is insufficient, the enterprise will not meet its objectives. At Warren Tech, the original objective was for each instructional program to support itself through school-based enterprise. The principal reports that almost all the programs have been successful, with the exception of those teaching office administrative support and accounting. The main reason that these faltered seems to be that their potential buyers were other businesses rather than individual consumers. Since the school is not located near other small businesses, these enterprises were not viable.

The type of enterprise depends heavily on the interests and know-how of the faculty and administrators involved. In many instances, the idea for the enterprise was the brainchild of the person who ultimately was given responsibility for the instructional aspects of the program. The superintendent at Mt. Edgecumbe tells how he first conceived the enterprise in his previous school district: "I've been a hunter and fisherman all my life, and so I started commercial fishing. The high school principal loved to smoke meats, so we got together and said, 'Let's put a program together here. Let's see what we can come up with.' He was a vocational teacher; that was his background. So we built a smokehouse, actually built it ourselves, bought a commercial smoker, set up a program, and we called [the program] Commercial Foods."

Success of the enterprise also depends on student interest. The enterprise teacher at Mt. Edgecumbe describes how some aspects of fish processing repel students:

> One problem that happened between this year and last year is a large drop in enrollment, and maybe that's one of the reasons this class is changing. The kids that were in the class got a lot of hassle about smelling like smoke and smelling like fish from other students, and consequently the other people [prospective students] found out about it and they decided that they didn't want to sign up because they'd smell like smoke and fish. So maybe if you're starting an enterprise, don't do something where you're going to end up smelling bad.

The Rothsay store developed in quite a different way. The town's previous lumberyard and hardware store, a combined operation, closed; the building was vacant for a period of time. One school board member, described by others as a visionary, proposed that the school reopen the facility as an operating business run by the students. He, the school principal, and a business education teacher discussed the possibilities. The school district approached the state board of education for a waiver to operate the business in place of the existing business simulation — a course that was included in the business education curriculum and was oriented to office occupations. Based on a market analysis completed by the teacher and on budget projections provided by the Small Business Administration, the district decided to proceed. A grant-proposal writer was hired and helped to secure external funding to start the enterprise.

In contrast to Rothsay and Mt. Edgecumbe, Belle Fourche provides an example of an enterprise conceived and planned by students. THIS, Inc., was developed as a result of the market research, demographic data, and other information gathered by students in a research-and-development course. Their assignment in the course was to develop an enterprise that would be owned and operated by the students in a school setting; they were not told what the nature of the enterprise should be. On the basis of their background research, they decided to develop and operate a school store and snack shop.

Avoiding Local Competition

SBEs must avoid threatening local suppliers. Rothsay had no competing businesses within the town itself, but there were potential competitors in other towns five or ten miles away. The instructor in charge of the SBE comments, "The grocery store, the implement shop, and some of the other existing businesses we found — we tried to never handle the same type of merchandise that they have, and we work hand in hand with all of them. We didn't try to drive anyone else out by stocking something they sold." As the principal explains, "You can't use tax money to compete against taxpayers. You can't go into a business . . . and compete with another existing business. You can't do it, because you'll kill them." Nevertheless, opportunities still exist for the Rothsay enterprise to make money. In connection with a local construction job, the SBE bid on a window project worth $28,000. The teacher pointed out that the only competing bidder was "from out of town, so there isn't anyone else here in town that's capable of bidding."

Other SBE retail operations also avoid local competition by not stocking items sold by other merchants. The Classroom on the Mall in Fairfax County has, for the most part, avoided complaints from other mall retailers (despite the fact that the enterprise receives rent-free space). During the second year of operation, the Marketplace had two complaints from other gift shops selling similar items, but the SBE buyers have been careful since then to avoid this kind of direct competition.

Restaurants, a common form of school-based enterprise, must also be sensitive to competition, because there are almost always commercial restaurants nearby. One SBE restaurant instructor warns, "This is a problem as far as the other restaurants around, because our prices are so low. It's like, you know, we can undercut. We would be stealing from them. So that's a really touchy area." To avoid arousing hostility, the SBE refrains from conspicuous advertising.

Even in Marion County, where the school has contributed to many community development efforts, competition is an issue. According to the principal, "This school has been operating since 1979. We've operated thirteen years. We've had one major complaint. That was the greenhouse," which posed a threat to commercial horticulturists.

The principal in charge of the Fairfax County construction program describes how that program accommodated local competitors.

> We don't have to work with unions in Virginia; this is a right-to-work state. We have no relations with the union. What we do have a relationship with is the Northern Virginia Builders Association. We don't compete with them, because we only build here in this subdivision, and the only thing we do is related-activity work. We don't go out and do any private work. We don't do work as any subcontractor or general contractor. If it's a community program project — for example, we did a job on Fairfax Station, a replica of the original train station. A local contractor provided materials, and we provided the labor. That's the kind of thing we do, and that's not competing.

In child-care services, SBEs must be careful not to undermine other local providers, despite the general shortage of supply. The director of one school-based day-care center comments, "They have a waiting list down here. But see, our prices are competitive, $42 per week. We don't undercut anybody. We don't try to undercut."

Avoiding competition with local suppliers is important, because a school enterprise operates under the legal authority of the local school governing board, which is accountable to the local electorate. The Rothsay principal thinks that their SBE "wouldn't have worked unless you had community support. That's number one. You'd be surprised how many people wait until 9:20 to be waited on by students. The majority of our business is done during the hours that the students are there. [People] like being waited on by the kids."

An administrator in the child-care program in Brooks County describes the important collaborative relationship with a key local agency: "We also work very closely with the Department of Family and Child Service and Foster Care. Sometimes they'll place a child in our day-care center and pay for it out of their funds rather than putting the child in foster care."

An instructor in the Fairfax County car dealership comments on how local commercial dealers themselves provide vital support for the SBE:

> Their feeling is they would rather have us train the students on the cars and then hire those students than worry about the little amount of work that we may take away from them. They find the students they get a lot more qualified and better able to help them. That was their whole support in this foundation thing. That is, "Look, we need mechanics, we're going to need trained mechanics, even college-bound mechanics to take care of our cars that are coming in the future. Let us help you. Let us set this up and let us get it in place. We want a good program, so when you send me a kid, he's able to

do some work." They're not resentful. They've helped us out. I can show you two cars back there that came down this week from dealerships that know what we work on down here. "Look," they said, "for us to do this, it's going to cost you [the car owner] this money. Why don't you either donate it or let them work on it at the school?" That's how they help us out with donated cars and things like that. But they've also helped us out with work that they know we can fix but that would be way too expensive for them to get into.

Setting Appropriate Prices

SBEs must balance several conflicting considerations in determining the price at which to sell their products or services. Setting a low price benefits consumers but may undercut local business competitors and create ill will. If demand is inelastic, pricing products too low also loses potential revenue for the SBE. On the other hand, if demand is elastic, the reverse is true: pricing products and services too high fails to maximize sales revenue, although it avoids threatening local commercial suppliers.

These conflicting considerations can produce complicated compromises. For example, Station KBLE at Gateway Tech charges very low prices for advertising: $.50 for a thirty-second commercial and $1 for a sixty-second spot. But the total amount of commercial time is sufficiently limited that KBLE does not detract substantially from the advertising revenue at local commercial stations.

At Rothsay the lumberyard gives a 5 percent discount to two local construction contractors who are supplied mainly by the SBE. This had to be approved by the school board. But as the only lumber dealer in town, the SBE did not have to worry about threatening other local suppliers.

Figuring out what price to charge can be an educational exercise for students. At the Fairfax County Classroom on the Mall, students work through a formal analysis of cost and expected demand to determine where to set prices. Instructors in this marketing program feel that this is a strategic part of what students must learn to do. Price competition with other local merchants here is not a concern, because the SBE tries not to duplicate what other stores in the mall are selling.

The Fairfax County car dealership also involves students in setting prices. When a car is donated, student workers estimate what must be done to make it marketable; they cost out the parts to determine the amount of money they will have to pay out; they review the blue book and newspaper advertisements; and they visit dealerships to determine the probable range of sales price for the rehabilitated vehicle. Using the cost information and the potential sales price, a decision is made as to whether the car should be repaired for sale, repaired only to provide practice, or scrapped for parts. Once work on a car is complete, the actual cost of repair is tallied. This information is used with data from newspaper advertisements and the blue book to determine an initial listing price. The students compute two prices, one high and one low. They start each sale by marking the high price on the sales tag, but they know how low they can go in negotiating with potential customers.

Finding Suitable Facilities

Some SBEs operate on the school campus, where they must compete for space with other programs. But the problems can be more difficult when an SBE is located off campus. The Fairfax County construction program, for example, operates as a full-time magnet school at a small remote site. When we asked students how they would improve the program, one said, "Bigger lunches"; a second chimed in, "That's what I was going to say." A third student explained, "They feed you elementary school lunches out here." The students were right. A teacher later elaborated, "There's a system in place which transports elementary school lunches in the district but no system to transport high school lunches. So the truck that takes lunch to the elementary schools which don't have their own kitchens stops here." The point is minor—it would be simple enough for the school system to obtain larger lunches—but the larger lesson merits attention:

creating an off-site teaching location is not a common occurrence for school systems, and maintaining standards requires extra attention. The problem is exacerbated when an SBE serves low-achieving students, as this one does. (It is difficult to imagine a school system building a small full-time magnet school and observatory at some remote location for its Advanced Placement science students and not providing adequate lunches.)

The Fairfax Classroom on the Mall has had better luck with facilities, but that program has also had problems. When the original mall manager left, negotiations with his replacement were necessary to ensure the program's survival. But this transition exercise has had to be repeated on six occasions! And at one time, the school system was asked to contribute $20,000 to pay for finishing the mall space that serves as the SBE's classroom. An influential member of the program's advisory board helped win the school board's approval for this expenditure.

Hiring Qualified Teachers and Administrators

Facilities are important; qualified instructors are crucial. Two major requirements for SBE staff are the ability to teach students how to run an enterprise and the ability to impart the technical knowledge and skills needed to produce the goods or services the SBE will provide.

The Mt. Edgecumbe superintendent comments on his problems in finding teachers:

> If I had to tell you what I have to do to train people who come in here in order to teach entrepreneurship. I think we maybe ought to have required them to have owned a business and failed. I think [such people] would be better teachers. People who teach entrepreneurial cottage industries need to be people with real business experience. And it doesn't really matter what subject matter they're in, because all of it can be cross-curricular. In this program, I've had a home ec teacher, a science teacher, a business manager — who isn't even a certified teacher,

by the way — an elementary teacher who's also our Chinese language teacher. So those are the four people that I've had in those programs. Totally diverse. It doesn't seem to matter.

In addition to entrepreneurial ability, the SBE teacher also must possess the specific know-how to create the SBE's product. Sometimes special certification is also required. The Fairfax County car dealership, for example, must be licensed (like any other car dealership in the state). Thus, in addition to instructors who can teach the technical aspects of automotive mechanics and auto-body repair, the Fairfax County program is required to have an administrator who can secure both a state independent dealer's license and a state salesman's license. When the initial staff person who possessed these qualifications left the program, the vocational principal had to study for and pass the necessary examinations to obtain the licenses. On the other hand, the instructor serving as site supervisor for the Coop Tech apartment rehabilitation project is not a licensed contractor, though he describes himself as having broad experience in construction. "My background is in carpentry and house construction. That's where I got my experience. Most of the work we're doing [on the SBE site] is the kind of work that we did, or I saw done, or I was involved with."

Instructors' legitimacy in students' eyes depends in part on their technical expertise. One student in the Gateway radio broadcasting program advises, "If you're going to invest in the good equipment, hire somebody who knows how to properly maintain it and is willing to correct the problems as soon as they arise rather than waiting until things get worse."

Qualified people may be attracted to an SBE because they prefer school working conditions to those in industry. The lead instructor in the culinary arts program at Metro Tech, for example, had previously worked for eight years (five years as chef and three years as sous-chef) at the Registry Resort in Scottsdale. One reason he came to work for the school system was that it allows him to work during the day instead of at night, as chefs often do; and he prefers to work days, because he has a young family.

Similarly, the steady hours and regular pay available in teaching appeal to some trades workers who have experienced the ups and downs of independent contracting. Some of them have long wanted to teach, and they can still practice their trade during the summer.

Recruiting and Selecting Students

SBEs have to "advertise" for potential participants. Then they have to decide how to select students from among those who apply and how to retain those who enroll.

Some SBEs are limited to single high schools — for example, Belle Fourche and Rothsay. Others, such as Fairfax County in Virginia and Metro Tech in Phoenix, enroll students from a number of high schools in large districts. In this latter kind of setting, students have to be attracted from other schools to the facility where the SBE is located. An instructor in the restaurant at Metro Tech describes the program's so-called sophomore tours: "What I do is shut the entire program down for two weeks. Then, in the gourmet room, we have a screen going. We put up displays of cold food, mirrors all decorated with canapés, hot food displays, and then we give an overview of what the kid can expect to earn when he gets into this business."

Most of the enterprises we visited have available to students some printed material that provides information about the enterprise and its role in the related educational program. For example, Student Auto Sales in Fairfax County is advertised as an important component of the automotive program, with a strong emphasis on how the enterprise gives that program an advantage over other programs in the district. In addition to printed matter, schools offer videotapes, films, slide-tape presentations, and live presentations to potential program participants. Postsecondary institutions often make these presentations at local area high schools, either in specific classrooms or at career fairs. High school programs in multi–high school districts work with career-guidance personnel at local high schools and junior high schools.

Students are admitted to or selected for SBEs in various ways. Some programs enroll significant numbers of special education students or students considered at risk of not completing high school. These students are often placed by counselors or administrators rather than enrolling on their own initiative. The Fairfax County automotive instructor points out, "One thing you may not realize: we have both ESL [English as a second language] students and LD [learning disabled] students, and a whole bunch of different students coming from different schools. One school for emotionally disturbed students sends us a lot of students. Students who just can't get along with other students will get along in our program and really mature and have a vocation, have a skill for something when they can get out of here."

The principal at the Fairfax County construction project muses, "Why do they come? Probably the number-one reason is because at their base school they haven't been successful. We can supply the credits for graduation, and they might decide they can learn a trade, learn how to do some work versus hanging around the base school and not graduating."

An instructor in the Metro Tech restaurant, commenting on how students were originally selected for his program, reports on what he perceives to be the role of the home-school counselor (and how this role is changing):

> Some of them just say, "Well, you're not going to make it here academically; let's just shove you over here to this vocational center." And that's starting to change. It used to be this way. I mean, my first year here, this place was a dumping ground. That's how it was. You had every kid, and they didn't want to be here. And we didn't really want to deal with it. But as the reputation of the program has grown, the quality of the students is getting better. Each year it's gotten better. But you're still going to have some that just don't want to be here and are doing it only for credit.

In contrast, all students at Thomas Jefferson High School for Science and Technology are selected for their high ability in math and science, and those who wish to participate in basic and applied research activities through the mentorship program must submit a formal application, including a written statement of the student's proposed research project. Applications are carefully screened, and students participate in formal interviews with prospective mentors.

A similarly rigorous approach is used by Belle Fourche to select students for the research-and-development course — the course in which students establish and operate the school enterprise, THIS, Inc. Interested students are asked to write a letter of application that includes a statement about what they expect to achieve from their participation in the experience. Instructors then review the application letters and choose the students. (Other criteria include grade level and communication skills.)

In the Classroom on the Mall, students must undergo an interview before they can work in the store. The interview is conducted by a student panel, which reviews the application form completed by the applicant prior to the interview.

Students in any given SBE may give different reasons for being there. At Mt. Edgecumbe, one young man explains, "The reason I chose this class is my family worked in Sitka in a small business. Our family is all into tourism, and I'd just like to learn more about business." Two other students took that same class due to the accidents of scheduling. One of them reports, "I chose this class because there wasn't anything else that fit into my schedule. But then it's a fun class; it's fun processing." The other says, "My schedule got messed up at the beginning of the year, and this was the only class that the hours were open."

Family influence on students' enrollment in SBEs is sometimes strong. Several students at Belle Fourche note that they were influenced by parental support and encouragement. One says frankly, "My parents pushed." In some of these cases, the parents are entrepreneurs themselves and apparently want their children to have some entrepreneurial experience in school.

At Belle Fourche, students are influenced by teachers and by the entrepreneurial spirit the principal is trying to develop in the school as a whole. One student describes teachers' enthusiastic recruiting: "Teachers come up to you in the hall and say, 'I'm starting this new class, and I'd like you to be in it, because you could really benefit from it and you can help the other kids,' and that's really encouraging."

A student in the Rothsay SBE explains his reasons for enrolling in terms that echo the educational rationale described in Chapter Three: "I did it because of the different change of pace. I kind of thought about going into business, but I'm more of a people person, not a machine person. I took accounting last year and enjoyed it. I just like working with people. Being down here is hands-on experience. It's nice to get away from class. You're learning the same kind of things, but you're actually doing the real work here. It's fun, and it's a different way of learning. It's a challenge."

Once enrolled, most students participate on a regular basis and carry out their responsibilities with little if any prodding from the teacher. They go about their business with more autonomy than in most conventional classes. Some students act inappropriately, however, and must be removed. For example, a teacher in one of the child-care enterprises says, "We've had students that we took out of child care because their temperament or attitude wasn't conducive to working in the day-care center." A school administrator involved with the program elaborates: "I can remember several instances where someone couldn't handle the decisions in working with children. Their way of dealing with it was always violent hollering, very vocal. In addition, they often wanted to do something other than what the teacher was suggesting, not following directions. So we had to remove them from the program."

Even among the carefully selected and academically talented students at Thomas Jefferson, problems do occur. The mentorship coordinator describes one incident: "This year we did have a problem with two students who should never have been in the program. They were very immature, and they went to Naval Research and they committed some security violations. They didn't enter properly, and they didn't have proper passes. One of them had a pass, and the other one didn't. She had a temporary pass and you're supposed to call in to get in, but she slipped in with the other one. It hurts, because they're a big firm. We're still talking about it. I'm afraid in that particular division they're not going to let the students back. [The employer] is judging the program by what the girls did." Yet this is a program in which students produce original research, and some of the students have even applied for patents.

Our case studies indicate that school-based enterprise is compatible with all kinds of students, from the developmentally delayed to the academically gifted, including both those who enjoy school and those who are dying to get out. But it takes effort to maintain high standards of achievement and behavior, no matter what kind of students there are.

7

Running an Enterprise
for Learning

As productive enterprises with an educational purpose, SBEs face a unique set of issues. In this chapter, we describe how SBEs have evolved instructional methods, developed curriculum, maintained student motivation, and coped with staff turnover. We also discuss the need for networking, the role of partnerships, and several inherent conflicts with which SBEs must deal.

Finding Methods to Encourage
Student Independence

Despite the widespread prevalence of SBEs, there are no preservice teacher education programs that prepare enterprise faculty, and until recently, there has been no in-service education available either. In the 1980s, however, both Foxfire and REAL Enterprises started offering support for enterprise activities in their networks. REAL sponsors a two-week teacher-training institute, an experimental activity-oriented curriculum, a teacher support system, and a state development program. However, most SBE teachers have not yet participated in structured professional development focused on the particular challenges and opportunities they face. Consequently, teaching in a school enterprise requires much improvisation.

The counselor who directs the Hollywood Diner talks about the requirements of his job this way:

> Ivan [the director of the school] is great support; he's always there when I need him, but he's not here all the time. And the cook's a great cook and a nice person, but she's not a social service professional. So basically, I kind of stick my neck out on a limb most days, and it's kind of interesting. I like it, but they never taught me that in college. What do you do when a kid does X? So I make it up. That's the way this program is working. You have to have initiative and creativity. If you take a person who's used to doing it the normal, conformist way, I think a program like this would be in serious trouble. Ivan's a very resourceful guy and very determined. I happen to have some creative ability in addition to my commitment to the kids. That's helped us a lot; it's gone a long way. If the program had someone who could never improvise or be spontaneous, I don't think we would have ever made it to this point.

Consistent with their own practice of learning as they go, SBE teachers frequently stress the importance of students' developing the capacity to think and learn for themselves. These teachers are aware of the need to prepare students for lifelong learning in careers that are changing with increasing rapidity. SBEs may be better designed to provide this preparation than most high school classrooms — and even many corporations. The principal at Thomas Jefferson High School notes that the mentorship program could not continue to work with one particular corporation, because that corporation did not understand the importance of encouraging a "learning mentality" on the job:

> In the end, [our relationship with the particular corporation] didn't work out because the notion of an

apprenticeship was still very much job-specific. What we kept saying was that over the lifetime of an employee, the job is going to change so radically that to lock in on job-specific training early is damaging. That may be more productive in the short run in terms of their learning that job, but you still have the problem that they have to learn a new job soon. More importantly, you're talking about a [job-specific] learning style that's inappropriate, and companies often don't understand the importance of learning style. So the learning mentality that employees bring to the job is very important, and [this employer] doesn't think so. The problem companies have is that they teach their employees to learn in a mechanical fashion and then ask them to do jobs that require more independence or ability to take on responsibility for their learning. So companies are consistently locked into retraining, spending more money in the long run retraining them than they would have if they developed the right learning style up front.

He goes on to point out that the schools themselves reinforce and reward the wrong learning style.

The way you get into this school is by testing well. The way you test well is to become pretty good at figuring out what the teacher wants you to know. When we sit down with freshmen and say that we want them to spend more time with ideas, to come up with questions that need to be answered, they often don't know what we're talking about. In fact, parents will come to us and say that we're not teaching their children. They want us to tell them what chapters they need to study. I think that there's more power in asking the students to work with the issues of design, understanding multivariate as opposed to single-variable solutions, of asking people how to use schools rather than simply teaching them.

How SBE teachers try to stimulate students' independent thinking is illustrated by the chef at Metro Tech:

> I won't just stand there and say, "Okay, now put in a half a teaspoon of salt. Okay, now put in a half a teaspoon of black pepper." Then I've got a robot in front of me. The kid is not going to learn. So I make the students constantly ask questions and get feedback. I try to make the students think. They'll say, "Chef, how much of this do I put in? Chef, how do I do this?" Then I say that I don't want a robot. I say, "So go make a French onion; I want two gallons. You've got an hour and a half to do it."

Students accustomed to conventional teaching are sometimes upset by such tactics, but many grow to appreciate the independence. One student says, "Sometimes it seems like the instructor is mad at me for not knowing what the problem is in the first place. What I have to do is go to the books. That might be his whole intention, for me not to rely on him but to go to the books. It sort of annoys me. You know, he's standing there and knows the problem, but he won't tell me. If he's not as helpful as I wish, I think that it's because he's just trying to get me to use my brain, to use common sense."

As students develop greater capacity to think on their own, they begin to produce new ideas. The chef at Metro Tech welcomes these. "The students that are really interested are constantly coming up with suggestions. I learn from my kids a lot. I've got one student who's really big on plate presentations, and he comes to me with ideas on how to do the gourmet room. And he's come up with some good ideas."

Given the scarcity of training programs for SBE teachers, it is not surprising to find enterprise faculty who learned their teaching tactics outside schools of education. At Rindge Tech, for example, the following interaction was observed:

> Chef Joel is crouched close to the floor, looking up at two students. Both are black—one African Amer-

ican, the other from the West Indies. The teacher is looking intently at Sammy, seemingly unaware that Keon is standing only a few feet away. His voice is low but intense. He holds a restaurant-sized can of vegetables with the sharp-edged lid still partly attached. "This is a very serious safety hazard," he says, staring into the boy's eyes. "You should never let something like this happen at a restaurant. It's too easy for someone to get hurt very badly. You can get very bad cuts from these. This is a serious problem." After only a few more words, Joel is gone, checking on someone else's work in the restaurant.

What happened in this exchange is more complex than is evident, as Joel explains:

> The mistake was really Keon's [the student who was observer]. Keon had opened a can and brought it to Sammy with the lid partially attached. He didn't realize the severity — that you could be really hurt by one of those lids. It's one of the worst cuts you could get, just rips you open. So actually I'm yelling at Keon, but I do it by yelling at Sammy. So Keon's not getting upset at me, because I'm not yelling at him, but he *is* getting the message. An old chef taught me that trick a long time ago. He said, "You want to tell somebody something, tell someone else. Works 100 percent."

Joel protects Keon's self-esteem, sure that he will learn the lesson better if he does not feel attacked and shamed. Meanwhile, Sammy feels that this is a passionate lecture about safety — one that he can take to heart; he trusts Joel enough to know he will not be punished for something he did not do.

As the chef moves around the room, working with other students, the teaching is very Socratic. Taking advantage of the presence of an observer, he encourages a shy Asian girl, "Tell him what you're doing here. Why are you making this? How is it going to be prepared?" Shy and feeling very unsure of

herself, she stumbles verbally. Joel says, "You know!" and proceeds to lead her, one phrase at a time, as she explains that she
is assembling portions of legs and thighs to be fried with red
sauce to make buffalo wings.

Watching Joel, one can see dozens of instances of one-
on-one coaching. Joel approaches another student cutting vegetables: "No, hold the knife this way," he says with a friendly but
rushed tone. He takes the knife, demonstrates the move, has
the student repeat the motion, compliments him, and then sails
across the room to someone else. One of the lessons that Joel
is teaching is that it is possible to move fast and be relaxed at
the same time. He always has time for a joke or wisecrack, always has time to compliment a student on something (even if
it is something as simple as managing to come to school that
day). He does all this while making it clear that everyone must
hurry to get lunch ready on schedule.

Unfortunately, few teachers are trained to *coach*. Joel was;
he was educated in a culinary school, where coaching is a common method of instruction. But most teachers are taught in classroom settings and have had little opportunity to observe coaching, let alone learn how to do it.

Joel also seems to have instinctively added the teaching
of all phases of the industry to his largely unwritten curriculum. He talks about bringing the idea to his present job from
his previous experience as a Little League coach. "With my Little
League team, I used to take a couple of kids and let them do
the roster. Not only be a player, but be a manager too. And
that's what we try to do with these kids: let them be the cashier;
let them come in and count the money. I have them receive;
I have them make the orders up on Monday. For example, I
have them make the phone call and place the order, as if they
wanted to be a food-service manager."

Participating in the operation of any SBE exposes students to the many facets of actual work. In the productive setting, students can learn to work cooperatively, think on their
feet, respond to issues, and deal with others. One student's
description of how much he had learned about dealing with customers prompted a classmate to interject with enthusiasm, "Yes,

that's called tact!" In addition to dealing well with customers, students learn to work well with each other. The fact that an enterprise must stay on schedule often encourages cooperative learning simply because of the need for efficiency. Informal peer tutoring is commonplace, and students sometimes even teach community members. In Marion County, the community development program placed students in the role of teachers with adult farmers as their students when they developed a demonstration fish pond.

SBEs afford many opportunities for students to take independent responsibility. For example, in Belle Fourche's writing program, the production of an anthology requires individual students to be responsible for different chapters. If a student fails to do the assigned work, there is no way to avoid public embarrassment. This program's teacher believes that it is important to keep the students' sense of ownership: "If that's removed, then all you're teaching them is, 'Gee, it's impossible to fail'; someone will always come along to ride in and save you."

The fact that SBEs exist for educational purposes means that teachers should try to give students the instruction they need in order to carry out their responsibilities. One student compares the patience of his SBE teacher to the attitude of those supervising his after-school job as a tile setter. "Out there [in the after-school job], if you do something wrong, you get yelled at. Well, you're not yelled at, but you're supposed to know the stuff. At school, the teacher teaches you one time, and if you mess it up, he'll tell you how to do it again."

But the stress of running a real enterprise can strain teachers' patience. Students at one site said that when their project got behind schedule, some of the teachers began "jumping on them" rather than modeling the correct way to behave on a job site. (Scheduling can be a problem, and some sites have developed strategies to avoid these crises; this issue is discussed later in this chapter.) And one student in a school restaurant, asked how he would improve the program, said, "I'd get a head chef that smiled every now and then." Another student added, "When he gets a new shipment and some of the material is missing, that's when you've got to watch out!"

If students are given real responsibility but insufficient time or support to fulfill it, they may simply experience failure, frustration, and resentment. On the other hand, if the responsibility is insufficiently real and demanding, students do not take it seriously. This seemed to be the case in the school-run radio station we observed. With no pressure to make money, students did not face the real-world challenge of trying to satisfy both advertisers and listeners. One of the staff commented on the distinction between the SBE and a commercial station: "They'd have more commercials to run, for one thing. There'd be a little more time pressure on them in getting required program material on the air. We just have a few spots, and even if we increase our advertising sales, I'm sure we're not going to have six spots at a break like a commercial station would have all day long. But in a for-profit on-the-air station, there would be more pressure in terms of the time and getting all these commercials in." Because of the absence of pressure, "you're too free here. That's the whole point. There are no logs; there's nothing to follow. You just go in there with the CDs. You can say anything you want in between; so naturally everybody tries to be funny, because it's their little piece of fame."

The Problem of Curriculum

One ubiquitous problem in SBEs is the absence of a ready-made curriculum or text for each program. Instead, the small group of teachers running the enterprise have to develop the whole scope and sequence of what students are expected to learn—a nearly impossible task. No one has yet developed even a generic curriculum for enterprise programs that could be used as a starting point. As a result, there are missed opportunities for learning even in the best programs. For example, at one of the school stores, a student worker who did not know the SBE's discount pricing structure misinformed a student customer about the price of doughnuts. After the customer left, the instructor entered the scene, and the student asked for clarification about prices. The teacher responded by holding up one finger and saying $.50; two fingers, $.75; three fingers, $1. The student nodded to indicate understanding, but there was no discussion of the reason for the pricing structure.

In some of the SBEs we visited, the enterprise experience seemed so rich that it did not occur even to the observer how much was missing. The child-care program at Metro Tech, for example, did an excellent job of integrating child psychology and hands-on training; the students learned a great deal of how to work with children. The center also modeled an excellent child-care program for them. However, instructors spent little time teaching the students about the child-care business. One advantage of an SBE is that teachers are free to teach all phases of the industry. But at Metro Tech (and several other schools) students learned less about some aspects of the industry than they would have at a nonschool job site. One student compared what she learned at Metro Tech to what she learned in a profit-making day-care center: "What I learned [in the school] was more of the safety regulations and first aid. I also completed my CPR here. I had a kid choke, and I knew what to do." But, she continued, "I learned a lot more in my outside work about how to run a business. I learned how they obtained insurance and what they went through to get kids to come in and what prices you should charge. I learned about city regulations and a lot about how much the school costs — utilities and things like that."

In the absence of ready-made curricular materials, SBEs sometimes try to adapt the teaching practices used by private industry in the training of apprentices. But apprenticeships often involve long periods of repetitive work; it is this that makes it profitable for the employer to provide apprenticeship slots. At one construction SBE, where students were learning to lay brick, the teachers — all professionals in the field — used as a standard the rules of their industry's apprenticeship programs, which state that it takes an apprentice two years of full-time work to learn the trade. But the students perceived what they were doing as highly repetitive; they objected to what they saw as limited faculty attention and inadequate teaching of techniques for unusual situations or use of other materials (such as stone). The faculty, on the other hand, felt that students were being trained for the entry-level jobs they might obtain: laying straight rows of brick. But apprentices who are trained in this way are paid, and students felt they should be too.

Although there is no easy answer to the ethical issue, the school could have reduced student discontent if it had spent some time training them on a wider variety of work skills. And students might have gained a sense of ownership had they been involved in more aspects of the construction process. This would have been difficult, however, since many of the students were sent to this SBE as a last resort and were not as motivated as those at other sites, most of whom volunteered for the program.

Coping with Staff Turnover

The character and interests of each key staff person strongly influence a program. When a staff member leaves and is replaced by another, the program invariably changes. In some cases, the replacement person cannot reproduce the energy and excitement of the program's creator. But sometimes a change of staff leads a program in new directions with significant improvements.

For example, the superintendent at Mount Edgecumbe describes how each new enterprise teacher modified the smoked salmon recipe: "I've trained teachers, but each one wants to go their own way. And so they keep horsing around with the recipe; and that's fine, because you've got to have some ownership. Even if I gave you a smoked salmon recipe and you thought it was fantastic, you'd change one thing so it would be yours. I mean, we all do that so we can say it's our recipe." This is to be expected: faculty create the program they desire, and a change in faculty means a change in desire.

This does not mean that programs cannot be continued under new "ownership," only that they cannot be reproduced exactly. When a program loses its director and a new person takes over that position, technical assistance and planning time should be budgeted in order to allow the new director to "change the recipe" and claim ownership of the program. Similarly, if a second site plans to duplicate the program from an established location, the new site will need technical assistance support as it decides how it wants to change the program.

Student Motivation

Every enterprise strives to win and sustain student commitment. This can be difficult, however, because students are young and have shorter attention spans and less ability to defer gratification than adults, on average. They may become bored if there is too little variety in the work. Juniors in their first year at the Fairfax Classroom on the Mall describe their initial reasons for joining the program: "Real people, real businesses." "I thought it would be fun. We got to go to the mall and get experience. Marketing class in school—all you do is listen to a teacher." In the kiosk: "We see it and we do it." "We do more physical things than verbal." But the novelty can wear off. As one of the teachers observes, after "doing it for years, they get bored with it. They have the enthusiasm at the beginning, but it peters out. So it's good at times to do something different."

For students in some fields, there is an established reward system. Students at Thomas Jefferson High School, for example, have the prospect of winning a Westinghouse prize for their work in science, and this can be valuable motivation even to those who do not win. For one student, a lesson was learned in losing: "I started out with the conception that I could [win] a Westinghouse, but as time went on, one of the things that I learned about research is a lot of this is luck—not plain luck, but luck is tied in. And luck wasn't on my side. The gene I was trying to isolate didn't really work." For students in more traditional vocational education areas, there is the chance to win ribbons in a wide variety of vocational education competitions. However, for many SBEs there are no national or community competitions.

The designer of an enterprise must think long and hard about what is needed to motivate students. Not every student will be motivated by the same device, of course. Some students will be almost self-motivated by intrinsic interest in their work. Child-care enterprises have an advantage in this regard. One young woman in the Metro Tech child-care center speaks exuberantly about working with small children: "It's just fun working with [children], because you can see that they're learning in their eyes, the way they light up when they understand something. They're learning every day, and it's interesting to watch them. It's fun." Another student interjects, "You feel good when you've taught something."

As we have noted, motivation varies from student to student; building in motivation depends on matching students' interests to what they are doing. For example, some students derive a great deal of satisfaction from lawn-mowing, and others are excited by brick-laying. But there are some students who find both of these tasks thoroughly boring. Having no intrinsic fascination in grass-mowing or brick-laying and no real perception that construction work is a possible career, some of the students participate merely because it is better than having to sit in academic classrooms all day. It is a way to get a high school diploma for students who are unable to tolerate only academic classes long enough to graduate. For these students — those lacking *intrinsic* motivation — the issue of motivation is more difficult. Once staff members have done the best job they can at matching the student to the right task (even if the fit is not ideal), they must then look for other motivational devices.

One strategy is to limit the amount of work that is boring. At Mt. Edgecumbe, the enterprise decided to cut back drastically on the production of smoked fish, in part because the work was boring and smelly. But when unpleasant work *must* be done, it is helpful to involve the students in its planning and allocation. Involving students in the task of motivating each other can be turned into a valuable learning experience. For example, one Belle Fourche student says, "We really had to learn to do some teamwork. There would be people in our groups who wouldn't do as much as the others. We had to learn to get them to do more."

At Mt. Edgecumbe, students devised a simple job-rotation system; they move from one work station to another each day (along the lines of volleyball rotation). Students can tolerate boring work better if the enterprise mixes that work with more exciting and fulfilling activities. In the automobile shops we visited, students were cheerful about the unavoidable sweeping task when it was handled as a natural part of the automotive repair work they had done.

Paying students is another motivational strategy. Coop Tech, for example, pays students minimum wage for the hours they spend working on the apartment building. This seems amply justified, especially since many students come from low-income families. Moreover, there are not many part-time jobs available after school for these New York City students, and any student who could obtain an after-school job would probably find it exhausting after a day on the construction site. Paying these students clearly solves the motivational problem that some aspects of the work (such as removing a 100-year-old boiler from under the ashes and debris of multiple fires) might create.

As we mentioned in Chapter Four, SBEs sometimes give students material compensation in some form other than cash. For example, the Southington school store pays for students to travel to DECA meetings. These emoluments also serve as incentives for students to work hard.

One of the most elaborate and inventive attempts we have seen to provide incentives is the team incentive structure at Fairfax County's Classroom on the Mall, which we touched on earlier. Students are divided into four departments, each responsible for one kind of merchandise. Teams are formally rated on all major aspects of their performance, including visual merchandising, ledger updating, data base correction, sales promotion, interactions with a "secret shopper," profit-and-loss statements, and training new employees. Some of these tasks are performed by the team as a group, and their performance is rated by expert judges, as a teacher explains: "The students had to plan the training program that was going to be conducted for new employees, so they had to go through the employee handbook and find an exciting and innovative way to pass that information on to students who were going to be the new employees. Each team had to cover all the major parts of training— for example, customer service, how to dress, what to do in a shoplifting situation, attendance, tardiness, scheduling. Within their presentation, they had to catch all the things considered to be important." Presentations are judged by businesspeople from the mall, including the personnel director from J. C. Penney. Another group task is preparation of a booklet on shoplifting prevention, to be used by employees and managers. One team's work was "really excellent. The [mall's] director of security asked if he could have it." For the sales promotion presentation, students "have to come up with some activity to promote the store for that particular opening. That's evaluated by the mall management staff. Two or three members of the mall management staff came down to evaluate the presentation."

One particularly important group task is deciding what merchandise to order for each department. The team's rating is "based on a percentage of what sold as compared to what they ordered, so that if they made some good buying decisions and had high sales, that's turned into a team score. The team that had the highest percentage of things sold compared to what they ordered" receives the highest score on this component.

Other components of team performance represent team averages of scores given to students for work done individually. For example, ledger updating—what the teacher describes as "keeping track of the daily sales at the store once it is open, keeping track of the payroll budget, and keeping track of how much is still left in the open to buy, by keeping track when invoices are paid and how much that leaves, and keeping a running total how much we have left for reopeners"—is done individually, "but their team scores are made up of their individual scores. I average those grades and come up with their team score. You want to have a good team score, so you do your part of the work." Similarly, data base correction entails giving the team "a printout of what was in the data base. Invariably, when you have a lot of student input, there are going to be errors. For example, many times we'll look over the inventory and we'll have negative numbers. These are real errors that come about in doing business." Likewise, completing the profit-and-loss statement requires each student to "go back and see how much we spent in payroll, what came in terms of sales, how much was spent on inventory, and determine if the store made a profit or not."

In addition to performance of individual and group tasks, teams can win bonus points. "For example, if they wanted to come after school to help merchandise the store or enter inventory into the computer, you would give them ten bonus points for any member of the team who came after school and spent a whole hour or whatever. One team just came and were awarded ten points for each hour they spent on the computer and other little activities, restocking the store. There was one who ended up with sixty extra points."

The two teachers at the Classroom on the Mall believe this team incentive structure has helped to motivate students. "When you have a bunch of teenagers together and you give them competition, they're going to get out there and do more." The explicit specification of what teams are expected to do also helps students see more clearly what they are supposed to learn from working in the SBE.

Incentives have their place, but one of the most important lessons from SBEs is that students can be strongly motivated by the work itself it it is organized properly. Students working in SBEs have (and generally feel) a level of responsibility to other people—whether their task is as important as selling an automobile or as seemingly minor as running a power lawnmower to maintain the grass—beyond what they would normally incur in a school setting. A Belle Fourche student remarks, "The responsibility you were given is so beyond what you can get in a normal classroom." A teacher in the Classroom on the Mall says, "I think there's definitely a sense of pride in knowing that they ran that store, and it doesn't necessarily take money to feel that sense of pride. That's something very few high school students get the opportunity to do." One of her students, in a separate interview, corroborates that point:

> We do and we buy and we pick out the merchandise we want to get. We do all the displaying. We do everything. The teachers are just there to oversee and make sure we're not messing up anywhere. If we are, they don't fix it. They tell us, and we have to fix it ourselves. At work [on non-SBE jobs] you report to someone else, and they take care of the problem; you're doing what someone else says instead of what you think you should be doing. At work [in a non-SBE store] it's nice when you have

a good day and sell a lot. But at the Marketplace [SBE], you start out wanting to work and wanting to be there and stuff because you're running the place.

Similarly, a Thomas Jefferson student feels that the real, productive work off campus "seems a lot more important than working in the lab [at school] on something that may or may not need to be done. In some of the labs, your teacher comes up with the idea and you have to work on the project. In mentorship, they gave me a list of about fifteen different things that they needed to get done between now and February. I worked on all of them for about three or four days at a time, then picked which one I wanted to continue with."

Conflicting Demands on School Enterprises

SBEs face conflicting demands. One way to conceptualize those conflicts is to think of the enterprise as serving several masters. The first master is the student, whose education is the main (if not the sole) reason for the enterprise's existence. But the enterprise must, by definition, have a set of customers, and they too have requirements. Moreover, just as commercial businesses have owners whose interests are distinct from those of the customers, SBEs also have "owners" — people who possess the authority to affect the size (and even the existence) of the enterprise, and whose decisions may be affected by how much money the SBE makes or loses. Legally, the owner is almost always the school board, which operates through the local administration — in particular, the high school principal — and other faculty. Outside foundations also have a stake in some SBEs. These various masters — students, customers, school board, administrators and teachers, other funding sources — may have conflicting interests. The enterprise must decide how to balance those interests.

Since there would be no point in having a school enterprise if there were no students, SBEs must put students first. But the effectiveness of school-based enterprise as an educational device depends on convincing students that they must work in the interests of customers. Illusion and make-believe can be useful ingredients in school-based enterprise. To paraphrase W. I. Thomas's often-quoted dictum, that which is perceived as real is real in its consequences. Even though there is no obligation for the school to be in the business of serving real customers, once the decision has been made, the demands become real and may start to conflict with students' educational requirements.

A striking example of this conflict is offered by the culinary program at Rindge, in Cambridge. An outsider looking at the program, seeing students hurry to feed customers and collect money from them, would tend to assume that the customers and their money are the program's raison d'être. But Chef Joel makes it clear that these transactions are only a means to make the instruction more effective for students. Without the commercial connection, he explains,

> It wouldn't be a true shop. I can't stand throwing away something. I'm not going to make something without a reason. Why am I going to make a batch of soup if there's no place for it to go or if it has no meaning? The kids turn to me and ask, "What's this for?" [Given the existence of live customers,] I can turn to [the students] in this place and say, "We've got to get this out of here; we've got to be ready for lunch." In fact, we don't. We don't have to open the door. I can always put a sign up that says, "Sorry, we're closed." But I want to create the pressure, because they're going to be faced with that first of all.

It is important to remember that Joel is a chef, not a would-be restaurant owner. Chefs sometimes become owners, but most are employees, who in turn have charge of their kitchen staff. In the case of most chefs, their business is better thought of as a subcontract between themselves and the restaurant owner, who is their client. Likewise, when Joel attempts to simulate a real enterprise, his concern is almost exclusively with the food preparation rather than the customers. He says about the teachers and outsiders who eat in the restaurant, "They're just lucky. They just happen to be in the right place at the right time."

When Joel is asked how much money the cafeteria takes in, he admits that he has never bothered to work out the calculations. He does not know his profit-and-loss ratio, unlike an entrepreneur who depends on the bottom line. At the same time, Joel accepts with relish the need to respond immediately to the demands placed on him by the principal or other people who want a meal prepared for a special meeting. Asked whether he anticipates that his enterprise will change in the next few years, he first says that he does not anticipate any change. Then he adds, "I believe we're just going to have to adapt if we need to. If we have to have a morning breakfast instead of lunch, fine. If we have to go to a buffet, we just have to adapt to that. That's what you do in the business anyway."

In these and other statements, Joel reveals how the back of a restaurant works: its client is in fact the owner of the restaurant, and at this SBE the principal plays that role in many ways. For instance, the principal feels free to walk in and say, "I'm having a special meeting three hours from now. Can you set up the dining room and feed us lunch?"

Joel's identification as a chef rather than an entrepreneur helps explain the most important decision in the history of this SBE: to stop functioning as a restaurant open to the public and convert into a cafeteria used almost entirely by school staff. The public restaurant, called Cantabrigia, achieved a huge public-relations coup when none other than Julia Child, who lived nearby, gave it a favorable review. But Joel was concerned primarily not about having Julia Child as a customer or about newspaper reviews but about his students; and he did not want them losing time waiting on tables when they should be learning how to cook. Perhaps that sort of decision is a luxury of the privileged: school officials in socioeconomically and ethnically mixed urban communities might very much want their vocational programs to receive a review like Child's. It seems a safe guess that Bill Staffa, for example — the director of the Hollywood Diner — would not have closed the restaurant. Nevertheless, the school's principal, Larry Rosenstock, did not reverse Joel's decision. Joel seemed to be thinking only about his students when he said, "We don't want any more customers. We're not going to go out and advertise. We're not going to send out a kid with two boards reading, 'Come eat at the Cantabrigia.'"

There is no need to reach a definite conclusion about Joel's motives, and we lack the evidence to determine whether students at Rindge benefited from the decision. The point here is that SBE directors have the power to make important choices about their programs, and those choices depend on how the decision makers balance the perceived demands of students, customers, and other stakeholders. Delivering a real product means confronting the pressures of real production with real customers who must be satisfied, but sometimes it is necessary to pull the enterprise back from production so that these demands will not overwhelm the learning opportunities. This need was clearly recognized by the principal at Coop Tech in New York City. He explicitly refused to commit his student construction crews to completing a job by a certain date, because he did not want them to miss opportunities for learning simply in order to finish the work by a deadline.

Similarly, the principal at Southington ruled out the possibility that the school store might take over the school's food service. In addition to the difficulty of satisfying the myriad guidelines governing school lunch programs, serving lunch every day to 1,400 students would swamp the SBE's learning objectives. "Although there are some places that have tried that — to have their vocational food-service program try to run their food operation — it doesn't work, for a variety of reasons. One of the major reasons is that the vocational food-service program has a curriculum that goes along with it. It's not as if all they're doing is feeding people every day. They're learning."

However, the Southington SBE teacher concedes that, in the school store itself, serving customers sometimes takes precedence over learning. At each cash register, there are two students, one of whom is supposed to be teaching the other and letting the less experienced student get some supervised practice. But "during the prime time, of course, when it's obvious we're getting buried, there's no time to practice."

The Classroom on the Mall instructor also regrets that getting the work done leaves too little time for learning.

> [Running the kiosk] is an extremely positive learning experience. They learn so much from it. The one concern that we have about it is that it does encompass a lot of the school year in terms of time. By the time you're buying and ticketing, and then break down the store and do physical inventory after, you've used up a lot of time. It doesn't give us a lot of time to teach so many of the other things that are so exciting in marketing. I'd like to have more time to do more case studies—really study H. Ross Perot, study Macy's, and maybe have more time to discuss where they went wrong, what they're going to do—and maybe have time to do a unit on discount retailing or green marketing. Just some of the more specialized things that are interesting. I can only touch on them for a day or two. I'd love to be able to spend a few weeks. There just really isn't the time.

Facing the same dilemma, a teacher at Belle Fourche is pained to relate how the pressure to meet a deadline can deprive students of opportunities to learn:

> We can do a garage in seven or eight weeks. That's if the kids work and the weather cooperates. It's a learning experience along with working. We're in kind of a bind now, where this last week the kids aren't getting much out of it other than "Put that there and nail it here," because it's got to be done. That's really unfortunate. It really turns kids off. You get to the point that, instead of helping them through something, you'll do the cut yourself so you won't have to do it twice, and you end up with a lot of kids standing around with their hands in their pockets waiting to be told to do something. And

that's a problem. That's what I hate about deadlines, but that's part of the real world. The only
other thing I could do — and I'm not sure that I
could do it — is say, "Listen, we're going to take our
time. If it takes a week beyond the end of school,
you're just going to have to come back and help
a couple hours a day."

Student schedules impose rigid constraints. In commercial manufacturing, and even more so in construction, the size
of the labor force may change drastically from one time period
to another. Workers are hired when the workload is heavy and
laid off again when they are no longer needed. Since a school
cannot do this, a school enterprise must find some way to maintain enough work to keep students busy throughout the school
term. Furthermore, unlike businesses, which are free to hire
workers for whatever hours they are needed each day, SBEs must
employ students when their daily school schedule permits (making sure that the period in the SBE does not conflict with other
classes students want to take).

Virtually every site in this study has had to grapple with
this problem. In Rothsay, the store shuts down in early May
so that students can be involved in taking annual inventory;
normally, this would be done during the summer. The store
also employs students from two neighboring school districts who
want the experience. Students from each school are scheduled
in the store for one class period (less than one hour) each day.
Rothsay students start at 9:24, those from the other schools at
10:14 and 11:12. Some students find this frustrating. One complains, "I don't like it at all. I would much better like to be able
to finish my work and know that I did a good job than just leave
it to someone else." The Metro Tech child-care center in Phoenix manages to stay open as many as fifteen hours on some days,
but each student works only two of those hours.

Just as the human needs of parents force a long day on
the child-care center, in some cases an inanimate product forces
its own schedule on the enterprise. At the Fairfax County construction site, one teacher tells about pouring concrete: "Pouring

is a problem, because we've only got one two-hour block to work in. Then I have to pull kids out of class to baby-sit the cement the rest of the day." The challenge is to make baby-sitting cement a sufficiently valuable educational experience to make up for the time lost from other classes. A similar challenge faces the Hollywood Diner, which is located some distance from the school but is required to serve customers throughout the morning, making it impossible for student workers to receive a full program of classroom instruction.

As one solution to the problem of students' limited hours, SBEs can provide customers with a discounted price to compensate them for adapting their schedules to the students'. This may mean focusing the enterprise on a specific clientele that has flexible hours. For example, the Warren Tech cosmetology program caters to elderly customers, who can come during school hours and can spend the extra time that it might take to have their hair done by a student. Similarly, Warren Tech's auto-repair shop — an enterprise chosen because of the educational value of the work to be done — keeps cars longer than a commercial shop would. They can do this only by charging much less than the market price, promising high-quality work, and serving only a small fraction of the total demand for their services. The construction enterprise at Coop Tech, on the other hand, provides its student labor at no charge to the low-income apartment owners; in exchange, it accepts no deadlines for completing work.

Other enterprises solve the problem by the choice of product or customer. The Southington school store sells only to students, who are available as customers at the hours the SBE students can work. Paquin School, which has its students for only a few months, selected products appropriate for an individualized sewing curriculum, which permits students to enter and leave the program at any time.

Teachers' time is also a constraint, as Southington's SBE instructor points out: "The store takes a lot of time. If you didn't stay late every day, I don't think it could be done. But what could happen with the school store is that teachers could let that become part of their psyche and say, 'Well, I can't do everything,' so the store becomes a problem. If you put the extra time in the morning, evening, Saturday, then pretty soon you're not going to be teaching kids anything." A state supervisor for marketing education conjectures that the need for SBE teachers to be flexible about their work hours may explain why there are not more SBEs in big-city school districts: teachers' unions there may be more aggressive in limiting teachers' unpaid work outside of school hours.

Part of the strategy for overcoming the limitations of students' and teachers' time and abilities is to rely on other staff members for both mundane administrative work and specialized technical tasks. School administrators themselves often pitch in. For example, the superintendent at Mt. Edgecumbe concedes, "I find myself ordering the sawdust and taking care of 100 other things in order to make it possible for them to work." Some SBEs find it necessary to rely on people who are neither faculty, administrators, nor students. Coop Tech, for example, requires its homeowner clients to do all the dangerous outside work on their five-story building rehabilitation. The Hollywood Diner hired a professional cook because it had no chef-teacher on its staff. The Metro Tech child-care program hires nonstudent workers, in addition to paying students to work during nonschool hours; these nonstudent workers are able to earn credit toward a professional child-care certificate. Rothsay hires paid employees to staff the store and lumberyard after school hours and during the summer.

Giving first priority to education precludes trying to maximize SBE income, because this would require more repetitive work. At Mt. Edgecumbe, the superintendent is very clear on this point: "We went in the hole every year. We were an educational class, and so our goal wasn't to make a lot of money. We didn't really need to even show a profit, because our goal was to educate students, and we tried to do that and make money."

Some schools do take seriously the small profits earned by SBEs, perhaps because in a highly centralized school system, those profits are among the only discretionary funds available. At one school where the vocational education program wanted the income, the enterprise operated a high-volume store

selling doughnuts and cookies, which provided little more training than is given in a fast-food outlet. However, the program
reduced the amount of repetition by rotating many students
through the store, so that it provided a small amount of helpful
work experience to a large number of students who had never
touched a cash register before.

Since school budgets usually depend on the number of
students in attendance, SBEs may help augment school revenues
by keeping students enrolled. For example, the director of Hocking College's hospitality program points out, "We lost about
$15,000 in the last fiscal year. It takes only one student to stay
for two years with the state subsidies and tuition to cover that
loss." This fiscal argument reduces conflict between education
and profitability, since both now imply putting the student first.
Again, though, the educational value of SBE depends on making students believe that it is important to serve the customer.
The Hocking administrator wrestles with this: "If you have the
choice between keeping the student happy and making the customer happy, that's a difficult decision to make. Tuition is $500-
some a quarter, and there's $3,000 subsidy per year comes into
play, plus a dormitory fee, revenue from the bookstore. . . . It's
rough."

If, in trying to emphasize educational benefits, teachers
give assignments that are not directly related to the work, there
is a risk of losing the element of realism that makes education
through production meaningful to students. For example, students at the Fairfax County construction site were asked to keep
a journal of their work. They saw this as something that they
were doing for the school, not for themselves or to get the work
done. One student said, "I think it's stupid. It's for [the English
teacher's] benefit, not ours." Another student elaborated, "The
purpose of the journal is for her to keep a record all day, all
year long. So people who look back will be able to say, 'Oh
yeah, they did such and such yesterday.' Or 'They raked grass
or built half the wall or put studs up this day.' Or whatever."
Asking students to write a journal was at one level a sensible
attempt to integrate academics and work—an essential purpose
of every SBE. Unfortunately, the students were also correct:

the journal was assigned at the request of the supporting foundation for some unspecified purpose. Since these students had almost without exception done very poorly in regular classrooms, it is not surprising that anything resembling regular classroom work at the construction site would be hard for them and would therefore require careful justification.

This illustrates the general danger that school-based enterprise can take students' work experience and make school out of it, so to speak. To high school students, being treated as a worker means being paid more respect and being treated as adults. The Fairfax County construction students, many of whom had had difficulty accepting teacher authority in the past, were concerned about this. One offered this suggestion for improving the program: "Instead of treating the people who are going to be here in the program like students, treat them like people who are working here. If you get mad at one student, you shouldn't punish every student you teach." Another echoed, "One student gets the teacher mad, so he's mad at everybody else." This prompted the first student to add, "I was told I wasn't going to be treated like a student; I was going to be treated like somebody who was on a real work situation. When I got here, I found the total opposite, and that made me really mad. I expected to be treated like somebody who was working instead of being treated like we were still in a regular school."

In addition to the risk of demeaning students by treating them as students, there is also the risk of demeaning them for the sake of public relations. In the case of the Hollywood Diner, this was the inadvertent result of trying to please the well-meaning foundation that provided initial financial support. The issue revolved around the restaurant's name. First it was called the Kids' Diner. This name stressed the restaurant's dependent status and appealed directly to the heart of social welfare–oriented foundations and individuals. (In its gentle way, it is reminiscent of the sort of names given to nineteenth-century private institutions — names like the Home for Incurables or the Hospital for Destitute Crippled Children.) However, it was not a good name for attracting customers, winning the support of the downtown Baltimore business community (which needed a name more in keeping with the flavor of the Baltimore renaissance), or attracting corporate contributors more interested in being associated with a going concern than with a needy charity. For these clients and customers, the Hollywood Diner was a better name. Presumably, it was also more acceptable to the students involved, although theirs does not seem to have been the deciding voice.

Just as the realism of school-based enterprise may be jeopardized by artificial academic exercises or clumsy public relations, it may sometimes be difficult to reconcile with community service. Private enterprises are not expected to be public-spirited, although they often are. On the other hand, a school-based enterprise operating as part of a public institution must serve the interests of the local public which is its constituency. Some programs that perform public service seem uncomfortable with that aspect of their work. When Metro Tech decided to have its construction students work on a house being built by Habitat for Humanity, for example, some staff members were unsure whether doing so would be a violation of the separation of church and state. And the faculty did not discuss the issue of service much with their students, apparently feeling that it was not part of the students' preparation for real work in the construction industry.

On the other hand, commercial enterprise and community service sometimes blend smoothly in SBEs. For example, Brooks County students and faculty participating in the REAL program decided to create a shoe-repair shop both because it filled a potentially profitable market niche and because the service would be helpful to the community. Similarly, the Paquin School not only makes money by selling toddler clothes, it also serves the black community by providing clothing in styles that African Americans appreciate but that are not widely available from white-dominated clothing firms. At Belle Fourche, one high school student's enterprise did its small part for regional economic development by producing clothes distinctive to the wind-swept state of South Dakota, featuring an artificial thistle stuck permanently on each garment.

One important form of public service in some communities is improving relations among different racial and ethnic groups. Bill Staffa, director of Baltimore's Hollywood Diner (whose students are nearly all African American), describes some of the complexities of racial politics: "Sometimes we get the kids who actually steal the cars and who are in for breaking and entering. But most of these kids don't have long, chronic, hardcore histories or offenses. They're good kids." The complications arise in dealing with various kinds of customers:

> We get a lot of black businesspeople coming in here, city workers — there are a lot of black city workers, state workers — and the kids see black role-model professionals. It's really neat. And the black professionals love to see the black youth working. I think black professionals get sick and tired of hearing about black kids failing. So if they see young black males in here working, the black people are going to respond to that and the white people may pick up on it. We have a little Greek old lady cook and a white Italian guy [describing himself] up front, so that helps. But sometimes they'll see only two employees, and they may both be black. However, there's nothing we can do about it. And as far as I'm concerned, there's nothing really that I want to do about it, except that I do wish that I had a little bit more mix so that we could just hold it up and say, "We're open to everybody." It's a problem, but at the same time, these guys, if they're good workers, they come over to the table, and people do lose sight of color. The white businesspeople have told me many times how pleasant the service has been. I haven't had any problems with white people.
>
> The only problem that we've had in here came from three black males who were drug dealers. They were rude, cursing at my kids; they were just a problem. My kids were completely offended. They wanted me to take over the table, and I wouldn't do it. I said, "You do it. You see me eat this stuff

all day long. I beg for money, I [put up with every-
one] who comes in here and tell them to come back."
I wouldn't do it. I told them, "*You* do it. You owe
it to the Diner; you owe it to yourself. You've got
to get over this hump, because people are going to
do it to you for many years to come. You're like
the rest of us, you know: until you get to be very
rich or very powerful, you're going to eat that for
a long time, in between good times. You're like the
rest of us." They understood. Basically, I forced
them into understanding. That's a program decision.

Staffa is more worried about potential discrimination
against his graduates when they apply for employment; he is
concerned that the Diner might be labeled as a minority training program and struggles to avoid that: "Well basically, since
I'm white and I'm wearing a coat and tie and I'm speaking
well — that's all [potential employers] see. I don't convey the image that I'm working with kids from the projects. I convey an
image of dignity and positivism. Something positive: 'We're
youth; we're working with youth.' We're not saying anything
about urban city kids. We just say youth. It's fresh. I would
never come out and say we get predominantly black males. I
would say, 'We're open to all involved, and they're accepted on
the basis of their desire to work.'"

Networking

Most of the enterprises that we studied have discovered the importance of creating a network of community supporters. The network provides customers for the enterprise, financial gifts, information about obtaining resources and about production methods,
and political support to impress the school board, if necessary.

But networking outside the school system itself is an area
in which many educators are inexperienced. While the superintendent of schools has ample reason to make contacts in the community and some school principals actively reach out to their
communities, most teachers have little time or reason to do so.

This means that they may underestimate the importance of a network.

Among the sixteen SBEs that we studied, we saw considerable evidence of the importance of networking. Sometimes that networking was essential to get an enterprise off the ground. Paquin School used its network to obtain most of its customers, for example. In Fairfax County, a network provided the basis for creating the Foundation for Applied Technical/Vocational Education. But networking offers ongoing benefits as well. The Hollywood Diner depends on its network for financial support. The cosmetology staff at Warren Tech and the chef at Rindge use a network to find employment for graduates. The school store in Southington uses a community advisory board to obtain political support.

The tale of Rothsay's store and lumberyard, as told by the school administrator, illustrates the importance of networks:

> Our lumberyard closed down about 1986 and sat there vacant for over a year. We didn't have any buyers. The school district started looking at it as a place for an industrial arts class, where we could store the lumber right on the shelves and have the boards sized right there. Randy [the teacher] is vocationally certified in many areas, so he's pretty versatile and we can shift him around from course to course. So we started thinking about that, and we decided, well, we're going to buy it. We bought the lumberyard for a potential classroom for storage, which we're always short of. One of our school board members, something of a visionary, was walking by there one day and he said, "Why don't you guys run that as a business?" And so he talked to Randy and Joe and me, and we sat down and started talking about it. Randy put together a curriculum pretty much, and I helped him with that a little bit. We decided that's possible, so then we contacted the state of Minnesota and, if we could get it up and running, they would give us a waiver

to run it in place of our business simulations class, where Randy did market analysis. [The Small Business Administration] did the budget projection. And a fellow out of Northwestern Hospital did a market analysis for us.

Then we hired a grant writer, Joel Mertz from Underwood, who wrote a grant to the West Central Initiative Fund. Originally, we wrote the grant for $65,000 for inventory and equipment and cash flow and getting the thing started. Well, they awarded us $30,000 for inventory only. So then we got some people together out there, some housewives and some other folks, and they went around and looked in different stores and picked this out and that out, and we went through a couple of suppliers. I don't know how many meetings Randy went to trying to line up the supplier before we could work out one that would meet the terms of the grant and work with our school district. That's an obstacle, because there are certain things that we didn't want to do and there are other conditions that we felt we had to have, like a return policy. If we had a dead item, we didn't want it taking up our inventory dollars and not move. We still got stuck with a couple, but for the most part it's been pretty good. We worked with the local bank, and he provided the initial cash flow for us when we got started. The Community Development Corporation sponsored us with some funds; I think that was right around $20,000.

Each school seems to provide a different example of how a network can be built, but one important factor is the personal charm and aggressiveness of the staff. A striking example is the work of Bob Yurasits, principal at Coop Tech. With his school located on the Upper East Side of Manhattan, he was able to turn contacts with strangers on the street into long-term client relationships. He describes one incident:

Actually, it was a chance meeting. I was going out for lunch, and he was going out for lunch. He was there and had just moved from the West Side, and they were looking for a place to store some of their props and stuff, and he happened to walk out as I was walking by, and he said to me, "What kind of a building is this?" And I said, "Who are you?" We started to talk, and the next thing you know, we had an agreement going, so I gave him a little storage space, and he said, "What do you do here?" I gave him a little tour, and he said, "Gee, do you think your kids would be interested in doing a little stage work?" So one thing led to another, and we got involved producing sets for the Shakespearean theater.

One of the lessons in this incident is that the educator should be always alert to the possibility of doing a favor for someone who might then return it in an important way. One does not think of a school as a good place to store a local theater's stage sets. However, the response of the principal in this case was to think, "He has a problem. What can I do to help?"

Other SBE administrators and teachers also excel at finding this kind of quid pro quo. An administrator at Hocking College describes how the wildlife management class helps out a state agency:

The wildlife area is some thirty miles from here. The entire class goes there and does practical, hands-on wildlife management practices on a real Ohio Department of Resources, Division of Wildlife area. Their people out there are helping to supervise our students. They're also getting work done. This is a way we can trade back and forth. [The teacher] said, "Do you think we can do this?" Sure we can do this! It will all come back in time. It's come back many times over before now. So sometimes it's trading labor; sometimes it's outright cash; sometimes we know down the road we'll need something. We don't know right now what it is. It's PR. In plain terms, it's, "You scratch my back, and I'll scratch yours."

Networks are built in part from the professional contacts educators may have developed from working in the field. These contacts can then expand a network through their own firm. Bill Staffa, for example, has connections to a major hotel: "There are about a half a dozen people at the hotel: the director of personnel, their executive steward, their executive chef. I placed my first kid with the executive steward. He's a personal friend of mine. Catering—that's where I know everybody from." The student in question turned out to be an excellent employee, but this was not the most important factor in establishing the Diner's link to the hotel:

> The hotel understands the value of the workers, they understand the value of the public relations, but at the very heart of it is this guy on the inside who believes in me because he knows I'm sincere and he knows I'm not going to abscond with money and I'm not going to quit. Okay, so basically his belief in me has fostered his own intense drive to get everybody else. He's the executive steward; he's not on the executive committee. He's not a real big shot there; he's influential because he's a good worker. Basically, he's drawn in everybody—I've addressed their staff—he's pulled it all together. The hotel is now a big help to us. Their engineers help us, for example.

Contacts in the field are important as potential employers of program graduates as well. At Warren Tech, the head of the cosmetology program is an important professional leader who has many contacts among the shops in the Denver metropolitan area. The auto-shop faculty at Warren teaches advanced workshops to auto-repair workers throughout the state, providing the enterprise with a valuable set of contacts and strengthening the reputation of the school.

Community groups or individuals may become part of an SBE's network of friends because they have an interest in the program's students. For example, Paquin School for pregnant teens has two natural groups of friends — persons committed to the women's movement and middle-class African Americans — who can often be counted on to help this project because of its strong gender and racial identification. Paquin has also been able to take advantage of personal identification — the response of individuals who themselves have an experience that bonds them to the students in the program. It is well known, for example, that the wife of a very prominent Baltimore politician is an alumna of Paquin, and she has not hesitated to provide help to the school.

This sort of personal identification may result from the quirks of history. As we noted, the Hollywood Diner was originally the set for the movie *Diner*. It therefore has a connection to some of the Baltimore businesspeople who were friends of the movie's director, Barry Levinson, and were the basis for some of the characters in the film.

Another source of network support is the contacts of enterprise partners. Again taking the Hollywood Diner as an example, contacts of the school's principal can be enlisted to support the Diner. Similarly, there is a potential (still unrealized) for Metro Tech to establish an ongoing relationship with Habitat for Humanity, connecting it in turn to important members of the religious community, whose support for Habitat might broaden to include support for the Metro Tech students who work with Habitat.

In establishing a network, SBEs can take advantage of the fact that they provide an educational service that many people would be honored to help. Julia Child published a laudatory review of Rindge's restaurant partly because she lived nearby but also because Rindge was her community's high school, educating the children of her neighbors. Not every celebrity will be so helpful, but the educator need not feel embarrassed about asking. Similarly, some individuals who work in government

and not-for-profit agencies want to serve the community but
find it frustratingly difficult to do so through their regular work,
given the everyday burdens and restrictions of their office. It
may be easier for them to provide a bit of help to another agency,
and they may derive personal satisfaction from doing so. It seems
likely that when Habitat for Humanity agreed to enlist Metro
Tech's students, the responsible individuals saw this both as a
good source of volunteer workers and as an opportunity to help
support a worthwhile enterprise.

On the other hand, in trying to establish ties to corporate
or institutional sponsors, an appeal to pure altruism may not
work. The director of the Hollywood Diner and the head of its
parent foundation describe how they have enlisted local corporations for their network:

> Public giving's incredibly tight now. I go to Block-
> buster Video because they're a video chain. For our
> big party, I'll suggest they loan us posters and card-
> board cutouts for the party, to decorate. Each fund-
> raising effort stresses a connection. Blockbuster, be-
> cause of movies. Coca Cola — we carry Coca Cola.
> And the hotel, because they get our graduates. We
> try to make the connection and then try to show
> these people how visible their contribution can be.
> We have an ability to really present their name in
> a good atmosphere.
>
> When we went out last summer to raise
> money, the only thing we had to stand on was the
> reputation of [the sponsoring] foundation. This
> place was closed. It didn't have a reputation for suc-
> cess. We might have paid a professional fund-raiser
> $10,000 without any guarantee of success. It's not
> the kind of thing that could be done by hiring some-
> body to help you put a direct-mail campaign to-
> gether. Our ability to raise money has to depend
> upon selling the idea to somebody who already
> knew what our organization had done in the past.
> Now it's different. I'm also trying to make this

new fund-raising letter say, "We don't need a savior anymore. We're offering an opportunity for you to join the bandwagon," although not in so many words. With other corporate sponsors and the commitment from [an important individual supporter, a connection through the film], suddenly we have something to offer.

A network can be formalized by creating a board of directors, trustees, or advisers. (If the board has actual power, as it might if the enterprise created a foundation to operate itself, it would be a board of trustees or directors. Otherwise, it would be an advisory board.) It is hard to overstate the importance of these boards. The head of the high-tech enterprise at Thomas Jefferson High School describes the importance of their advisory board in getting the school's technology labs started:

> There were twelve to fifteen on the board, I believe, and they were usually the presidents of the technology and scientific firms of the area. They were the people who provided the support for getting the labs started. We had places like TRW, Honeywell Research, and I don't remember the name of all of them; but the big firms in the area were mostly involved with it. Some of them provided equipment for the labs, some provided money, some provided resources or consulting and gave direction on how the labs should be set up.

The enterprises in Fairfax County are served by a foundation that provides vital financial and political support. The Fairfax Foundation for Applied Technical/Vocational Education had the advantage of having a very successful member of the community working to establish the board and using his own name to enhance its prestige, in addition to contributing his own money (and thus by example encouraging others to do likewise). In addition to this foundation, the Fairfax Classroom on the Mall also benefits from the marketing education advisory board, a group the teacher calls "high-powered." They meet monthly. The original idea for the Classroom on the Mall came from this advisory board, in fact.

The marketing education program at Southington, which includes the school store, also enjoys the sponsorship of a strong advisory board; it reviews curriculum, raises scholarship money, and judges student competitions. "They also protect us," the teacher says gratefully. "Recently, there was a plan put forward to put an addition on the school. Part of the plan was to take one of our classrooms away. Our chairperson, who is a downtown merchant who runs a collectible store, and another one who is on our committee wrote letters expressing their concern about the possible adverse effects on our program." These letters helped save the program's space.

In creating a board of directors or advisory board, enterprise initiators must think carefully about what services the board might provide and what its impact upon decision making might be. (The Fairfax County foundation board was built carefully to include an architect, an engineer, a real estate agent, and others who represent expertise in the various aspects of home building.) Most boards also need representatives of higher education institutions, because many graduates of SBEs go on to further education. Boards may need persons with political influence as well, in case a controversy about the enterprise arises. A good attorney is also useful. And professional educators from outside the school district can help ensure that student interests are well defended; they can also support local educators in the event that the board considers placing unwise demands upon the enterprise staff.

Partnerships

One of the more significant developments in local government during the 1980s was the spread of partnerships between government agencies and private firms, not-for-profit groups, and other government agencies. For example, the director of the Chesapeake Foundation, which operates the Hollywood Diner, describes its partnership with the school system: "We're a 'provider' or 'vendor' agency. The state contracts with organizations like us to provide services for their kids, and in this state there's a tremendous movement under way to privatize everything."

Big-city high school principals have become experienced in writing proposals and negotiating contracts with other organizations. Our sixteen SBEs include many examples of partnerships. Coop Tech's construction project is a three-way partnership, linking the school with a group of low-income homeowners and a government agency. In Phoenix, students helped build a house through a partnership with Habitat for Humanity; others operate an on-campus telephone reservation center for a motel chain (with the prospect of possible employment after graduation); and still others apprentice on campus in a private hair salon. The Fairfax County schools created their own partner in the form of a private, not-for-profit foundation. The Hollywood Diner is itself the not-for-profit partner for a city agency trying to make its downtown area more interesting and provide training for high school dropouts. It also serves as a partner for the Department of Juvenile Services, providing education and training for troubled juveniles.

Entering into a partnership can help schools work around their own bureaucracy. School principals can talk at length and with passion about the horrors of dealing with their central administration. Decentralization and school-based management have been developed in large part to deal with the problems of centralized administration. In one district, which is "self-insured" against injury claims by students, the principal describes what happened when one of his students was hurt at school:

> [The emergency room in a nearby hospital] charged him $400. He brought me the bill. We had an accident report form that we filled out. With students, you don't forward it; you just keep a copy of it at the school and forward it to the medical division only if the student wants to take action. About a month or two after the accident, the kid brought me the bill. So I said, "We're not going to pay the bill in the school. What we'll do is forward the bill

with the accident report down to the medical division." Almost two years went by. The guy was getting bills and bills, and each bill got higher. They were adding interest and now this $400 bill grew up to $1,600 in over two years. I called the medical division. They said that they had no record of the thing being sent. For them that's an easy way out. So I sent them a faxed copy within three minutes of the conversation. So obviously I didn't make it up. It was dated, signed, and everything else. The student had to go down there for a medical evaluation, over two years after the thing happened. Now it's in the fourth or fifth year and it *still* hasn't been paid. But the medical division is now checking out with lawyers and everything else. They've got people on it now that are investigating. They had people come here to interview teachers about what happened five years ago on such and such a day. Nonsense stuff. You see, that's why I say that self-insured really means no insurance.

In contrast, when this school sends students to an off-campus construction site, the contract with the property owner strongly urges that the owner's liability insurance be extended to cover the students.

A second advantage to a partnership is that it can provide a way for the school to handle large sums of money with an efficient accounting system. Most schools have a burdensome accounting system designed to protect the school against financial mismanagement. In Fairfax County, the foundation itself serves as the fiscal agent; it handles hundreds of thousands of dollars each year from the sale of houses and automobiles. The proceeds are used to buy materials and equipment for existing SBEs, and occasionally to start new ones. The schools themselves remain detached from all this cash flow. As a vocational program director explains, to finance the first house, "all of the foundation's [board] members went and signed their name on it as a charter foundation and took the loan out themselves.

Fairfax County, on all these houses out here, has no money
tied up in materials or land or anything dealing with that. They
just pay teachers' salaries." In Phoenix, the partnership with
Habitat for Humanity gave students experience in house building without requiring the schools to become involved financially.
They could rely on Habitat not only to negotiate the red tape
of home building but also to handle all material purchases.

Another benefit of partnership is the advice that partners
can provide. The Mt. Edgecumbe fish-packing enterprise teacher
cites Sitka Sound Seafoods as an example:

> They've been good to us too. They've helped us a
> lot in our product development and working with
> the Japanese. They also have Japanese people over
> there who go back home, and then they'll come over
> here and they'll bring me packages because they
> know I'm interested in packaging. They bring me
> back samples to taste, and I can see what it looks
> like. I take it over to the kids, and we go through
> it. So they've been helping us for years. There's a
> good relationship there.

Similarly, the Fairfax County foundation board includes professionals with the expertise needed for construction of new homes,
and the Hollywood Diner enlists executives from the restaurant
chain to provide technical assistance on marketing, advertising,
and a host of other activities.

The principal of Thomas Jefferson High School testifies
that new ideas derived from their partners in the mentorship
program help sustain the school's intellectual vitality:

> Clearly, the thing that sustains us is the long-range
> exchange of ideas that the mentorship provides.
> That provides in-service for our faculties. We're
> educators and we know school, but we don't know
> industry. As new ideas emerge in industry, we can
> keep up with them. We can't do that by going back
> to schools of education. We have to go into the field,

and the way to do that is through our students. They go out and we spend a year monitoring their work, learning about their projects and the work they do, and we become better informed.

Talking about in-service, there are other forms. We ask our companies to share with us the papers that they develop, and we work with their employees in terms of technology transfer and training. They invite our faculty to participate in formal training that takes place in their work. When there are conferences in town, the companies will make sure we get tickets so we can send the students and teachers to not only be there to hear the papers delivered but interact and mingle with the veterans.

We develop still other linkages with business and industry. There are examples of shared resources. For instance, we worked with the phone company to develop a new phone system in our school because the old one wouldn't handle the data. One of the reasons they were willing to become involved is that they realized that by locating equipment here, they could use it to train their own people. They could save the money on sending their people to California and wherever training had been taking place. It is also cheaper to rent the equipment — $200,000 — into this school and train people here than it is to maintain [another] training facility.

The partnership arrangement allows an enterprise to combine the expertise of two different organizations. In order to supply a product or service, a school-based enterprise must be able to carry out all the different functions of a business. Yet the enterprise is typically far too small to have specialists in all aspects; it resembles a corner grocery store. The vocational education teacher must see to it that all the different parts of the business can be carried out, ranging from buying materials to developing a market plan. In the case of the Fairfax foundation, the house-building program can depend upon the foundation to deal with such difficult issues as producing acceptable architectural plans at the beginning of the project and finding a buyer at the end.

A partnership with an experienced not-for-profit organization provides a school with the ability to organize a proposal and staff a new project quickly. The director of the Chesapeake Foundation, a not-for-profit partner to the Baltimore public schools and several city agencies, describes the foundation's talent:

> One thing with our organization: we're at a point right now in our history where we've got some really serious people. Despite the fact that we're a small organization, we have a half-dozen people who are very versatile. This gives us our competitive edge if we need to pull together a proposal. We have people within our ranks who could get a new project off the ground, even though it might be fairly well removed from their current job description, so we would have a grace period to hire the right person to run it for the long term.

No school has either the luxury of several proposal writers or the flexibility to move its staff about so quickly.

Despite their important advantages, partnerships also introduce problems. One great liability of the partnership structure is that it may tempt the school to avoid teaching those phases of the industry that are handled by the partner. While building a house for Habitat for Humanity has advantages for Metro Tech students, they are not involved in the drawing of the plans, the obtaining of building permits, the purchase of materials, and the selling of the finished property — all of which would be valuable educational experiences and a part of what one must learn in order to be a successful contractor. This is not an insoluble problem, however. The school can assign an educational role to the partner.

A second major problem is that the partnership creates yet another place where there can be a breakdown in communication and coordination. An instructor in the Fairfax County car dealership tells of such a breakdown:

> We had the Adopt-a-Student [program with a local dealership], and it didn't go very well; it didn't last very long. It went well when it *did* work, where a student in his senior year could go work at Tyson's Ford in the summertime or he could work after school for two hours. You know, just to see how their big dealership went. And we're not doing it now. I think we've had a change in who ran the dealership. [The new manager] has got his feet on the ground; this is the first year he's taken over there. So there are a lot of things that will come back, but right now we're kind of on hold.

Coop Tech stopped dealing with Catholic Charities after several years of helping that agency build low-income housing, because the not-for-profit partner was slow to provide materials, making it difficult to schedule students' work. However, we did not hear many stories of this kind. Apparently, schools and their partners in our sixteen SBEs have generally been able to sustain a positive relationship.

The creation of a partnership with a private organization, especially a profit-making organization, raises the possibility that the school will be exploited. In business, as in other spheres, a good deal of self-serving activity takes place. The Rothsay school administrator complains,

> The biggest problem that we've had, and I think it has to be solved in the future, is the supplier. There's a two-way street there, of course, and you have to get with someone who works. . . . The school likes to make as much money as we possibly can, get their balance out of it as quickly as possible. We'd like to increase our inventory. By having

more inventory, we'll have more sales. Well, I think when this contract expires with [the supplier] now, we've known each other long enough that we have to sit down, and I think we have to work out a better set of terms in what we're getting, because I think he's reaping more of the benefits and more of the profits than we are. And I could give you some examples: he's making more on a stick of lumber than we are!

However, we have only one unhappy story of an enterprise being financially harmed by a partner: the Hollywood Diner discovered the hard way that it did not really need a partnership with an expert consultant. Originally, the Chesapeake Foundation bid to run the Diner in partnership with a consultant recommended by an executive of a highly respected firm. The consultant would operate the business side, while a foundation-hired psychologist would train the students. According to the director of the foundation, they found a psychologist who knew the restaurant business as well:

We put an ad in the paper. We were looking for a case manager to work with the kids. Bill Staffa applied for the job, and he had the perfect combination of work experiences. I honestly believed that he would want to take advantage of his strong background in food service. He got very excited about the prospect of getting in at the first. As things turned out, the consultant was incredibly territorial, and from day one he didn't even want Bill in the Diner. It was like, "I'm running the restaurant," or "My people are running the restaurant. You take care of the kids." It was ridiculous, and I guess we probably spent the better part of two months trying to smooth out that relationship. The consultant got humble very quickly when things weren't working and some of his own people were leaving and weren't producing. There was an incredible amount

of animosity between this guy and Bill. I'm a firm
believer that this guy thought that fate would hand
him a business on a silver platter, and that's basically why he got into this. There was a minimal
amount of effort — no risk in terms of capital. He
would basically get all the credit for making this
thing work. All the state and city workers would
patronize it, and it would be great.

In fact, the consultant left the Diner bankrupt, and Bill Staffa
replaced him as director.

The Hollywood Diner is now careful to avoid unneces-
sary partnerships. For example, it never uses outside catering
firms when it rents the Diner out to special groups, instead paying overtime to its own staff. The Diner had held only one
event — a "sweet sixteen" party — at the time of our visit, but Staffa
sees catering as an important part of the Diner's financial future:

Oh, this place is so beautiful. We can host parties,
and they can lead to social connections, fund-raising
connections, not to mention that we could make
more money on one party than we can make in a
week. The cook and I and the two students worked
the ["sweet sixteen"] party. These guys know how
to get around the city by bus; they've been doing
it all their lives. They were out of here by midnight.

   If an outside caterer comes in, all we get is
the rental fee, and we get a bunch of strangers
traipsing around in our Diner. We have a full
kitchen of equipment. When caterers go to most
off-site locations, it's a bare kitchen — counters and
sink. There's nothing in it. The caterer has to bring
everything in. It's not the owner of the catering
company, but the employees. When the caterer
brings his own knives, he's more apt to verify that
everything's still there when his employees leave.
Employee theft in the restaurant business can bank-

rupt you, and that's why there are deaths with fires
where back doors are locked—because they don't
want people taking food out the back door and hiding it for someone else to come by and pick up.
Caterers have this problem with their employees,
but we don't with ours; our whole objective is to
get our kids to feel they have some ownership in
this program, so we eliminate a lot of that theft.

The wise enterprise leader will think carefully about select-
ing organizations with which to establish partnerships and will
evaluate continuously how those partnerships are working out.
The Hollywood Diner fully discovered its error only when its
first partner left town, leaving the organization bankrupt. In
that case, the enterprise partner was at least incompetent and
perhaps unethical. In the case of Coop Tech's unsuccessful partnership with Catholic Charities, the partner organization was
highly ethical but the partnership still failed. For whatever reason, Catholic Charities was unable to make timely delivery of
the materials the students needed to do a rehabilitation of a
homeless shelter, and the school withdrew.

It may be useful to think of the SBE as a partner with
the school that is its host. The enterprise and the school have
a common interest in providing the best education possible to the
students. However, they have subsidiary interests that may be
in conflict, so a clear contract between the two may be helpful
to both the enterprise and the school. Without some explicit agreement, teachers in the enterprise are in permanent competition
for resources with other faculty at the school. In a vocational
school, the debate about which enterprises are most worthy of
support goes on continuously. The same debate in a comprehensive school may be much more difficult to resolve, since the
enterprise may look much like an orange in the midst of all
the apples of the academic programs, with no sensible way to
weigh them against each other. The head of Southington's SBE
describes the relationship of the program to the rest of the comprehensive high school:

You have to get a good working relationship with
the support staff—that means the custodians and
the secretaries—because in their own way they control a lot of things that we need to have done, and
if you establish a good relationship with them, eventually they'll take action for the person that they're
working for. The second level is the faculty. That's
tough, because faculties are fragmented in many
different ways. There's the academic versus vocational. By the way, the vocational ones are not the
biggest ones to back you up. They're jealous. Within
your academic teachers, you have a split. You have
your extending faculty, who are involved with the
yearbook, the language club, who are club- and kids-
oriented. Then you have the teachers who say hello
when the bell rings and good-bye when it rings
again. You never win those people over, but you
can foster a good relationship with the involved
teachers. You do favors for them, and they'll do
favors for you.

He developed an artful argument to justify allocating $15,000
to his program over other programs. "It all depends on your
sales pitch. My sales pitch was, 'Listen, you've got sports teams
that compete, and you're putting in thousands of dollars.' The
sports director . . . told me that it cost something like $3,100
to put a football player on the field. I said, 'Listen, what's the
rationale to do this? These kids are in marketing education, they
compete, and if they win the right to go on to a national or state
competition, you say there is no money. You don't do that to
sports.' That's how we sold it."

This SBE leader has been very adept at forming partnerships within the school. He has joined forces with special education in organizing a venture with a local supermarket that
will employ special education students; he makes the school store
available to other campus organizations for fund-raising; he
financed the school's new fax machine.

The strength of school-based enterprise at Southington

is enhanced further by the fact that there are several SBEs. In addition to the school store, there is a vocational agriculture program that sells floral arrangements and plants, a child-care program that runs a day-care center, and a food-service class that serves gourmet meals for the faculty on a regular basis. As at Metro Tech, Hocking College, and other schools with multiple SBEs, Southington High School has become accustomed to the idea.

Even at these institutions, however, the SBEs are all attached to vocational education programs. In fact, nearly all existing high school SBEs have originated in vocational education. The most conspicuous exception is the Foxfire project, which published a series of books and magazines as an extension of an English class. Among our case studies, Mt. Edgecumbe and Thomas Jefferson High School are also exceptions. But for the most part, SBEs in high schools and two-year colleges have seemed a more natural application of vocational than academic subject matter. Vocational education faculty are also more likely to have access to production facilities at school. The restriction of school-based enterprise to vocational classes is unfortunate, however, because—as described in Chapters Three through Five—the benefits of school-based enterprise can extend far beyond the acquisition of job-specific knowledge and skills.

The possibility of using school-based enterprise in other subjects is appealing. Many nonvocational teachers know how to produce various goods and services, and a substantial proportion of high school teachers hold part-time or summer jobs outside of teaching. This implies that there is a great deal of untapped talent that schools might enlist in starting SBEs. To do this would require the school to provide resources in the form of start-up capital, facilities, planning time, and technical assistance. This resource support is perhaps the thing that it is most difficult for a public school to offer. When the city of Baltimore put the Hollywood Diner up for bid, no public school was interested, even though there are presumably dozens of Baltimore teachers who are would-be restauranteurs or amateur chefs and would enjoy running the Diner. Instead, according to the director of the Chesapeake Foundation, "There were six entities that came to a prebid conference. Marriott Hotel was one of them. The Carroll County [which does not include the city of Baltimore] Association for Retarded Citizens came. A couple of small-business people came. In the end, we were the only ones who submitted a bid; it was a joint venture with us and the consultant. The only thing I knew about the restaurant business was from my own college work experience as a waiter or busboy. I did a little cooking."

How can the resources that schools have, such as teachers who know the restaurant business, be mobilized to work with students in SBEs? One approach might be to organize in as many communities as possible both some sort of foundation and a technical assistance center to provide support. Individual teachers or groups of teachers might write proposals. Costs could generally be kept low, especially if social pressure were brought to bear by the foundation on the school district to provide release time. In general, the net operating costs of the programs we have studied have been relatively low once the initial equipment has been provided. Even programs that do not have a product to sell, such as the home-building programs in New York City and at Metro Tech, are nevertheless able to transfer many of their costs to clients.

This issue of how to stimulate formation of SBEs, especially outside conventional vocational education, is discussed further in Chapter Nine.

PART FOUR

The Future of
School-Based Enterprise

8

A Tale of
Two Schools

We have described how SBEs in various settings are preparing students for a range of possible futures, both personal and societal. Some SBEs prepare students for demanding four-year colleges. Others enable students to obtain skilled work after high school. Most SBEs appear to build students' capacity for learning through work—a capacity that is likely to become increasingly valuable as working conditions and careers keep changing at a fast rate. In addition, some SBEs give students experience in designing their own organizational forms and practices, seemingly helping to develop an understanding that should also become more useful as work organizations reinvent themselves with increasing frequency.

All of these apparent results are achieved by SBEs that, with a few exceptions, occupy only a marginal position in their host schools. In most schools that implement SBEs, only a small percentage of students participate; and those students who do participate spend only a fraction of their time in SBE activities. The SBE is often attached to a vocational program and usually does not influence instruction in academic subjects.

It seems likely that school-based enterprise would produce greater effects if it operated on a larger scale and with a wider scope, involving more students for a larger part of their day. To help envision what this would mean, the next sections of this chapter present two mythical schools: Veblen High School, located in a decaying urban center, and suburban Crystal Lake High School. We follow fictional students and teachers for a day and consider what that day might be like if SBEs were the rule.

Veblen High School: The Buck Starts Here

If Veblen High School played football, team members would probably be called the Bucks, but Veblen, in downtown Cleveburg, is too busy replacing Dewey with Deming and Drucker. The school is nicknamed Enterprise High, and the students are too wrapped up in their work to miss football.

This is the story of a day in a high school whose faculty and students are committed both to school-based enterprise and to using the community as the school. From Veblen, where all students participate in school-based enterprise, some students will go on to four-year colleges and some will not, but there are neither separate instructional tracks nor programs with condescending labels.

Robin Smith has thirteen-month-old Justin over her shoulder and is trying to burp him while she eats breakfast in her mother's kitchen. A single parent at age seventeen, Robin cannot wait to have an apartment of her own. She is training to be a medical secretary. This morning she is trying to read about possessive pronouns in her textbook. Her grammar class is difficult, but she has found out how important it is to write clearly and with a style that is acceptable in the business world. At school Robin works in the transcription center, which is one of the SBEs, and she transcribes some very jumbled and incoherent dictation. By using what she has learned in her English class and her medical terminology class, Robin feels that she has already picked up some saleable skills.

Howie Szabo, a Veblen senior, is the lead student in the transcription center. His role is essentially that of a shift supervisor. While Robin finishes breakfast, Howie is at the center assigning tapes for transcription and logging the jobs. The center is well equipped with networked laser printers and both PCs and Macintoshes, purchased from SBE revenues.

Students at the transcription center this morning are grumbling about the new time-card procedure. One student from the accounting class is trying to explain to her peers the advantages. Flipping back her headset, another student retorts that all the advantages are for the accounting team; the procedure is just a nuisance to her. The accounting student withdraws, unable to tell whether they will follow the procedure or ignore it. She is beginning to realize that good accounting practice is of little interest to the transcription center. She makes notes in her journal and plans to bring the issue up in the next accounting class.

It is surprising how many students are already busy in the center at 6 A.M. The marketing class, in its early research, found that one-day processing, with transcripts available at the start of a business day, had maximum appeal to the customers, so that is the program's goal. Students who work the early shift are paid a wage bonus. The delivery service that initially handled the transcription work turned out to be unreliable, so the carpentry class built a kiosk for the downtown mall where customers can drop off and pick up work. Students enrolled in the microcomputer support specialist program provide computer support and training for the center. Hilary, a senior in that program, is trying to install a network upgrade with no success.

Robin Smith says good-bye to Justin and to her mother, who will take Justin to day care later. She climbs on the bus hoping to study, but there are no seats. Robin never used to care about grades, but after listening to a presentation by the head of recruiting from a large insurance company nearby, she realizes that some employers are starting to pay more attention to them.

If Veblen's principal, Dr. Victor Pendergast, had not personally sold the concept of school-based enterprise to the insurance company, the transcription center would not exist. He persuaded the insurance company to provide liability and other insurance for all of Veblen's SBEs at a nominal charge. He also triggered enough interest to have an underwriter come to school and give a talk to the business students on the issues involved. Victor was able to add the insurance company to the list of sources to be contacted when it was necessary to do needs analysis for course offerings and their content.

Victor Pendergast's degree is in educational administration, and he has a knack for creating partnerships between the school and other organizations. He enjoys drumming up support for SBEs, but he is not involved in their day-to-day operation. Today he is at work early preparing a speech for a symposium. He has tentatively titled his talk "The Power of Pedagogy" but is dissatisfied with that choice. The speech is designed to explain school-based enterprise. He is emphatic about school-based enterprise as a fundamental philosophy rather than an add-on to the curriculum. He knows how easy it is to start up a venture and have it die two quarters later because the teacher is reassigned. He believes that school-based enterprise should be viewed as a new way of conducting education, not as another fad. In talking to business and community leaders, he must allay the fears of businesses that the school will be head-on competition. Ironically, he finds it easier to convince the business community of the value of school-based enterprise than the academic community.

Donna Cruz opens the regular weekly status meeting of the business integration group (BIG), which coordinates Veblen's various SBEs. At this week's meeting, a student will be presenting the issues surrounding profit, not-for-profit, and break-even philosophies. These weekly meetings are generally large (and often unwieldy), because they are open to all students. This student participation was very hard for some of the faculty members to accept; they struggled with letting go of their power. As Veblen's assistant principal responsible for curriculum, Donna oversees the operation of SBEs. The demands of monitoring the enterprises almost overwhelmed her until she created BIG, in which students solve many of the problems themselves.

Robin Smith walks down to the transcription center to start her daily two hours of work. She gets course credit as well as pay for these hours before the start of the regular school day. School-based enterprise is not just a part-time job to Robin;

it is the practice laboratory. She finds the reinforcement of the material in her medical terminology class very helpful. She is getting an A in that class — a grade that she has never had before. She likes the fact that the students run the business and that there is constant discussion of the work and workplace. She admits that she does not know why the department store where her mother works is not like this. (Her mother has never heard of Deming.)

It is lunchtime — 11 A.M. — for Pat Odegaard, the instructor in auto-body repair. This class operates the More Bang for the Buck body shop, located a block from Veblen. Today a student is interviewing Pat as part of the needs analysis of a marketing campaign for the shop. Pat is almost as responsive as his pet welding machine, and the student is flustered. Finally, he just agrees with anything the student says, and she goes away wondering if many customers are this difficult. Pat is not sure that making everything a business is a good idea; he wants to do what he was hired to do: teach bodywork.

One of the major problems the school encountered in starting the More Bang for the Buck shop was the outcry from many local shopowners, who objected to the potential competition and the unfair advantage that Veblen's low pay might give the enterprise. Knowing Pat, and the quality he demanded, made them worry that a lot of business could be lost. Victor Pendergast came up with the current concept to allay their concern. Pat and his staff select cars to be refurbished. The students then do all the work, including mechanical and electrical work and bodywork, to return each car to a close-to-new condition. Some of the cars are donated, occasionally one is a customer car, and some are purchased by the enterprise. About ten to twelve cars each year are refurbished this way and then resold, with no threat to the commercial body shops; no lucrative collision work is siphoned away. Actually, other body-shop owners have become full supporters since discovering the high caliber of worker the program is graduating.

As Pat eats a sandwich in his office, his door open for accessibility, he watches a senior student from the sales and marketing course out in the showroom with a customer. He listens

as the student shows the prospective customer the computerized log of the 1986 Malibu in the showroom. The student is
trying very hard to close the sale, but the prospect decides against
it and leaves. The student thinks back to several discussions in
his sales and marketing class, but he still feels that he has failed.
He takes out his project journal and starts to make notes.

Hernando Carrera, another Veblen teacher, comes to
Pat's door. Hernando is concerned about Peggy, a special education student with a mental disability and considerable speech
problems who works part-time in the auto-repair shop. Peggy
tripped on a hose and sprained her wrist two days earlier but
told no one. Hernando wants the other students to mentor her.
He worries about her working in the shop. Hernando himself
is deaf, but he lip-reads so well that few people are aware of
his disability. He remembers the horrors of high school, remembers that he was told to stay home because he would not be able
to learn. He now has a master's degree in special education.
He agrees to let Peggy continue in the auto-body class because
she has a talent for finicky paint jobs and will have a good chance
of finding paid work in a body shop on graduation. Pat agrees
to tell the students to keep their eyes open (and reflects on how
school has changed).

Robin Smith is now impatiently sitting in her business
mathematics class while the other students debate what projects
to work on next quarter. It irritates her that the teacher lets the
students choose, and she wonders why Veblen teachers do not
just take charge. She has mixed feelings about the course, partly
because she is somewhat behind and partly because it is rather
unusual. She has always liked math drills and practice, but in
this class everything is part of a project. Next quarter they are
talking about doing an analysis of credit-card bills, utility bills,
and mail-order merchandise. This so-called consumer analysis
project would teach the math that business uses in dealing with
customers. Robin never wanted to know any of this, but she
journeys on. She will try to do what the teachers ask her to do,
even if that means being part of this group decision process.

Victor Pendergast uses some of his lunch hour to polish
his speech. He changes the title to "The Power of Productive

Pedagogy." He needs a starting quotation and thinks of Charles Woodward. He suddenly realizes that it is time for the class he is teaching this quarter: business perspectives in education. Today he plans to talk about educational policy as set down by the state. Last time he did this, the students were surprised at the financial impact of such policies. They had not realized that school, state, and business together formed an interacting trio.

Donna Cruz grabs a few minutes during her lunch break to work on a graduate school research paper: "Learning Linked to Production." She is not satisfied with the title. The paper describes the curriculum sequence at Veblen: review, first project, second project, third project, and then internship. She wonders which course is the best example. She decides on history, as it is unusual for a school to make that subject overtly practical (as Veblen does). She also finds that it fits well into a cognitive psychological model and is a good illustration of using the community as a textbook.

Lunch period is also the time for today's meeting of the urban survey project, taught by history instructor Judy Malevich. Veblen High School is located across from the Franklin Mall in a "revitalized" downtown that seems very tentative in a commitment to its own revival. The school is housed in the old mechanical arts high school, which was extensively remodeled about the time it was converted to a conventional high school. The urban survey project, which meets after school or during lunch, was Judy's idea. She describes the project as "observing the obvious" and "noting the ordinary." In fact, the project has immersed students in the community's history. Her groups walk around downtown and observe. Once the observations have been made and consolidated, questions are asked. Judy listens to the findings and herself asks questions, such as, "Why is the old warehouse not being used?" At first the answers are simplistic, but as the group talks, answers are left behind and complex questions emerge about accessibility, safety, energy consumption, and living standards. Possibilities for the warehouse are discussed today, as the class considers preserving the past as their legacy to the future.

Some of the urban survey students plan on attending college, others are solid students but do not intend to go to college right away, and a few others are just scraping through high school. The project carries extra credit (after much negotiation with Victor Pendergast), which appeals both to high scholastic achievers and to students who, having fallen behind, need to make up credit.

Donna Cruz changes the title of her paper again to "The Power of Pedagogy Linked to Production." She reflects that Veblen's psychology course lacks an emphasis on cognitive psychology. Such an emphasis would help the students understand their learning environment and the instructional strategy. Victor interrupts her reflection to remind her that a group of visitors from Austin, Texas (including that city's mayor), are due any minute. The group's interest in school-based enterprise has triggered their visit, which Victor has encouraged. He is concerned that he should not have asked Tim Haldeman to address the group, however, given his prison history.

Tim, who teaches welding and works in More Bang for the Buck, spent three years in jail for running a chop-shop. He can weld anything, and even Pat says he is good. Tim says if he had known how to run a regular business, he would still have his own shop. He welcomes students from business, marketing, and accounting in the body shop, because he wants them to help expand the enterprise. After school, he sometimes works in local body and metal shops, keeping up with new techniques. He likes to say that the school shop should always be on the cutting edge.

After her lunch, Robin Smith goes to a communications meeting of transcription center employees. The center's instructor is very good at listening, helping but not interfering. Robin finds it very pleasant to have her opinions respected. The discussion today is about the problem of bad writing and grammar in the tapes and whether they should correct them. The consensus is that they should not, but someone suggests asking the marketing project students if such a service could be sold. The instructor suggests that they also contact the English teacher and have her students critique some of the transcriptions. That way, the transcription center employees can make an informed decision as to the difficulty of editing a customer's work.

Jonathan Peters is lecturing to the advanced mathematics course. Most of the seniors in the class are college-bound. When he came to Veblen several years ago to teach, Jonathan was both surprised and turned off by the SBE activity. He was used to teaching mathematics with a very heavy emphasis on the conceptual and on underlying structures. He saw no relevance or application to the accounting classes. ("Spreadsheet 101" was his contemptuous dismissal.)

When the students asked him about potential projects, he was taken aback; this was not typical. His response was to ask that brief proposals be submitted. Most of them were not worth any effort, but Sheila had proposed to reformulate the school district's enrollment projection method using Markov processes. A second student had asked about simulating traffic flow. Slowly, as he became more aware of his own biases, he began to see the links to the community. He and Judy Malevich have discussed the possibility of student math projects that might help her urban survey group.

Tim Haldeman is a hit with the visitors. He talks about school-based enterprise creating a new community vision. He sees school-based enterprise as giving students a choice that is healthy, diverse, and nonjudgmental. If the student chooses to study shop, that student is not blocked from advanced mathematics. Tim talks about the classroom walls disappearing and project orientation being the complete instructional method. He quotes an article about Deming and mentions that he wants the quality circle and total quality management movements to be the models for this new school. To Victor Pendergast's relief, Tim pronounces *pedagogy* correctly.

Jeanette Catinell is obviously very nervous as she places her notes on the podium. A senior in marketing, she explains to the Austin guests how the whole of Cleveburg is considered a textbook. Marketing students observe and ask questions in ninth grade. They identify services, opportunities, and needs as part of their tenth-grade work. In eleventh grade, they are the workers; but in twelfth grade, they can be the managers and planners. Jeanette's enthusiasm is obvious, and she is not using her notes now. Victor is pleased at the integrated view she has and realizes that he may have underestimated the students again. Recalling his own first exposure to this approach at the Rindge School of Technical Arts in Massachusetts, he wonders why it is still not common practice.

Elizabeth Langley, director of curriculum for the Cleveburg school system, provides the visitors' closing address: "The Power of Pedagogy When Used to Link Learning and Production." She traces the link between cognitive psychology and the SBE systems. Her position is that school-based enterprise is an ideal structure in which to implement the findings of the cognitive psychologists; other systems impose too many constraints. As Elizabeth describes the integration of the curriculum and the movement away from the discrete, compartmentalized "subjects" of English, history, and so forth, Victor realizes that Judy Malevich is really doing the curriculum design with her urban survey project.

After school Judy Malevich walks past the mall into downtown with eight students who are not happy to be out in the intermittent rain. The new social studies teacher is along to learn the observation technique. Judy points to the tops of the buildings, many of which have the building's date and original owner carved in their old stonework. She points to the date on a manhole cover and raises questions about a sewage system ninety-three years old. The students are completing an occupancy survey and hope to establish a pattern shared by failed and departed businesses. A student asks, "Why don't we interview the owners of these businesses?" Another student comments that if they find out why businesses have failed, they might help other businesses, which would be a tremendous accomplishment for a high school.

Robin Smith goes home on the bus. She stops off to get Justin, and they head home together. As she feeds Justin his dinner, she thinks about what she will do next year when she graduates with a high school diploma and certification as a medical secretary. She no longer minds school the way she used to. Sure, there are still drugs in the lockers and knives in the parking lot, but it is not all boring, and the teachers do not get on her back the way they did in junior high school. Maybe that is because she is grown up now, and they cannot treat her like a child. Justin burps.

Crystal Lake High School: Community as Curriculum

If the Crystal Lake Mallards had not lost to the Hamilton Crusaders by a score of 79 to 2 the year before Dr. Dorothy McClellan became principal, school and community interest in athletics probably would not have faded. It would be much more difficult to argue that the success of school-based enterprise at Crystal Lake was a substitute for athletics rather than a coincidence. But the new principal brought both a rush of enthusiasm and the concept of school-based enterprise. She started incorporating school-based enterprise into the curriculum and making the community of Crystal Lake the "living textbook" for the school almost right away.

Crystal Lake is thirty-five miles from the city limits of Cleveburg, beyond the suburbs but not quite rural. Because of the economic impact of the large city so close by, Crystal Lake has difficulty with its identity and its economy. What growth has occurred in the generally stagnant metropolitan area has been located mainly in the inner suburbs, but the new shopping malls are not easily accessible from Crystal Lake. The town has 4,821 inhabitants, 283 of whom are high school students.

Dorothy McClellan earned her doctorate from Teachers College, Columbia University. She grew up in Abbidale, North Dakota, a community of 12,000 people, and was determined to spend most of her career in metropolitan areas. However, she found that rural education needed her more. She came to Crystal Lake with a clear vision of the school's role in restoring a rural community.

Robert Smith gets up at 5:00 A.M. to study. He is getting a C in his math course, which is less than satisfactory. He takes a mug of coffee down to the basement so that he can do a math drill on his personal computer. The computer is an old one that he fixed up at very low cost. Before studying, Robert "chats" for a while on an electronic bulletin board and thus reaches out beyond the community. Such networks may be the nucleus of Crystal Lake's future, since they extend the town's physical boundaries through electronics. But Robert is not aware at this time that he is part of the redefinition of Crystal Lake.

Robert is eighteen years old. This is his fifth year in high school, and he expects to graduate in June. He fell behind because he flunked English and had poor attendance in his freshman year. He is very reserved and has found that his strength is in the diagnosis, repair, operation, and programming of computers.

Reluctantly, he signs off from the bulletin board and starts his math drill. When it is complete, he logs on to the mathematics department's computer at school to transmit the results of the drill for credit and grading. It is close to 7:30 now — time to catch the bus that will take him to school for his first-hour mechanical and electrical skills class.

Dorothy McClellan is in her office at her word processor at 6:30 A.M., preparing her presentation as incoming president of the State Education Association. This featured address to the state convention is tentatively entitled "The Power of Technology and the Power of Cognitive Psychology." Dorothy scrolls back to the title, stares, frowns, deletes it, and returns to her text. She writes, "It is important to understand the necessity of achieving what Beck called 'parity of esteem' in the high school. We can no longer accept the concept of separate academic and vocational tracks and the associated, though often unstated, belief that lower performance is acceptable for those interested in the manual arts. Instead, we must create an educational framework for activities that engage the entire cross section of students." She thinks for a moment and then continues: "The traditional vision of separate schools and classes for mental and manual workers has an appeal because it is simple and neat. Uniting all students, from the slow and recalcitrant to the academically gifted, is undeniably more complicated. But it is the only way to meet the civic and economic challenges of today and tomorrow."

Glenda Barry is Dr. McClellan's assistant principal. She is at her computer sending e-mail messages to the various SBE managers. Glenda's attention to process complements Dorothy's preoccupation with structure. She grew up close to Crystal Lake and knows the community well. After college in California, she worked as a waitress and as an executive secretary, then went back to graduate school for a master's degree in education. Now she has almost completed a master's in business administration. She came to Crystal Lake with a particular interest in distance learning and other educational applications of computers.

Glenda turns next to writing the agenda for the next integrated SBE committee meeting. This committee is the overall management group for SBE activities at Crystal Lake High School. It originated with Dorothy as a status-reporting group, but Glenda is trying to give it a real management function. She hopes it can provide such services as consistent mission statements, guidelines for introduction of new businesses, and other support functions. All faculty members are encouraged to serve on the committee in rotation, because SBEs are seen as a necessary part of the whole curriculum.

Robert Smith is looking out the window as the bus turns into the school parking lot, and he sees the shop where he is apprenticed. Al's Circuit Center is the bright, modern, electronic repair shop where Robert works and trains after his three hours of class. Al's motto is, "If your trans-is-tor has become a trans-was-tor, we can fix it." Al's Circuit Center, which has been in existence for two years, represents a turning point in Dorothy McClellan's SBE program. When Al Margolis was in school, he showed skill in electronics and a lack of interest in English and history. Rather than let Al drift into a series of low-skill jobs, Dorothy McClellan made a deal with him: if he completed all the course requirements for graduation, she would help him establish his own shop. Thus Al was set to become the first spin-off from the Crystal Lake SBE program.

Al's teachers gave him assignments that helped him plan his business. Now he has his diploma, and Crystal Lake has a new repair shop. Residents no longer need to drive to a large warehouse-style operation that sends their equipment away and several weeks later announces a $45 estimate charge. And Al's Circuit Center has found a ready market in the community.

Customers are coming from the surrounding area, even as far as Cleveburg, because of the personal attention and prompt response they receive. The businesses have also found Al to be exceptionally responsive when called to repair older equipment that the manufacturers want extremely high rates to maintain. With Robert Smith's help, Al is expanding to the world of personal and small-business computers (in part because the economics class did a trends and issues study for the Cleveburg area and stressed this as a major opportunity).

At the moment, Robert is nearing the end of the mechanical and electrical skills class. During the portion on mechanical skills, he is fidgety and bored. He sees little use for light welding and makes that point to the instructor. She responds that one of the skills that she found most useful in her six years in the military was the ability to repair equipment under almost any conditions and at almost any time. As she strikes an arc, she tells of being called recently to repair a printer that put out paychecks. There was a terrible snowstorm, and the service representative could not get through. She put a temporary (if ugly) weld on the printer's frame, which allowed it to continue working (still to this day) and meet the deadline for the paychecks. Robert does not use the word *grudgingly,* but that is how he accepts her explanation. Then he heads off for English with Mrs. Broadbent.

Emily Broadbent is sixty-one years old and represents the classic tradition of English grammar teachers who cherish the well-placed subjunctive, abhor the split infinitive, and view incorrect spelling as the grossest of poor manners. However, she understands the evolution of language and accepts change with resignation. She is waging a personal campaign to ensure that humanity conquers machinery and does not become its slave or victim. She is no electronic Luddite; she approaches a word processor as a tool to promote writing (though not as a substitute for language skills). Her particular emphasis in this quarter's writing class is the documentation of computer applications. She has made her English class very much aware of both the necessity for, and the too frequent lack of, good documentation. *Output* is still not a verb in her lexicon. She has a group of seniors analyzing e-mail communications to determine if the use of electronic media is reducing the clarity of communications. She plans to present the results as a paper, "The Power of Pedagogy in Overcoming the Weaknesses of Automation," at the next State Education Association meeting. She is thinking about changing the title as Robert Smith and the rest of her next class walk into her room.

Six years ago, the *Hamilton County Leader* ceased publication, leaving Crystal Lake without its county newspaper and without the *Crystal Lake Gazette* as its weekly insert. The *Gazette* documented those last, declining days of the Mallards, among other events in the ebb and flow of Crystal Lake life. The print shop was closed by its parent company; the manager moved away, and the shop sat there with dust gathering on its equipment and on the remnants of bills advertising stock sales. Interestingly enough, it was the home economics teacher who uncovered the latent need for a print shop and recommended to Henry Latitiere that its business potential be reevaluated.

Henry Latitiere is the polar opposite of Robert Smith. He teaches marketing, sales, business English, and career development. He has a deep tan, a BMW, and a certain flair. His transition to teaching was somewhat surprising after his successful career in sales (he "retired" from sales as lead representative for one of the country's largest chemical companies). But his competitive drive gave way to a desire to help students move into sales. He recognized that students who show strong social skills, who would welcome the personal interaction of the sales process, and who would be challenged by the responsibility of a sales quota are ill served by the traditional high school—an environment geared toward developing skills that stress the quiet, the studious, or the dextrous.

Jennifer Taylor is talking to Henry Latitiere about Font & Chase, Ink., a school enterprise that now runs the printing business. Jennifer is the lead sales senior at the print shop, and Henry is the faculty adviser. Jennifer gets academic credit for the time she spends selling and for revenue generated. She describes her experiences in a weekly report that includes graphs and statistical analysis. She makes enough to put herself through school; since her parents live on a farm almost fifty miles from Crystal Lake, Jennifer stays in town and pays board and room. She is enthusiastic and has been instrumental in forming Font & Chase, Ink., into a successful business.

Jean Comstock, the home economics teacher, prepares for another community survey class. She reflects on the somewhat convoluted path that resulted in the reopening of the print shop as Font & Chase, Ink. It started when she took a group of young students to interview people in the nursing home as sources for a history of Crystal Lake. This was a joint project with Louis Clark, the history teacher. She hoped that such a project would produce in students an awareness of the values and standards of the older generations. The resulting student monograph described the values that were the source of both the decline and the strength of communities such as Crystal Lake.

It was at the nursing home that they met Thelma Kaminiski, who emphasized the virtue of students' working. Thelma had come to this country from eastern Europe with almost no education. As a result, in her later years she became education's most enthusiastic promoter. But she insisted that the academic subjects be tempered with the disciplined practicality she had learned from hard work. Her family had worked for the *Hamilton County Leader,* and she continued to believe that a newspaper was an essential part of a community, helping people keep in touch, recording local events, and speaking to local worries. She kept coming back to the topic of the print shop as an example of how hard her sons had worked and how the shop used to serve, and should serve, the community.

Louis Clark then interviewed Thelma's "boy" Leo Kaminiski, who had been the typesetter for forty-two years at the print shop before retiring ten years ago. He pointed out that there was still a strong demand for services if upgraded technically with laser printers and the proper typesetters. Louis also talked to Leo's brother, Kurt Kaminiski, who had been the *Hamilton County Leader*'s press man. He was less enthusiastic about modern technology, but he pointed out that the older machines that still sat there were more than adequate for producing bills, envelopes, and paper sacks that could be sold in Crystal Lake (and far more cost-effective for that purpose than the newer technology).

Louis Clark and Jean Comstock went back to Dorothy McClellan, who saw the print shop as a possible venture for the newly created Crystal Lake High School Enterprise Foundation. The shop's corporate owner had given up hope of finding a buyer and was willing to donate the shop and equipment to the foundation as a tax write-off. The Kaminiskis contributed $3,000 to refurbish equipment and buy materials. Font & Chase, Ink., now prints forms for the school district and town government, as well as advertising bulletins for local businesses. Kurt and Leo Kaminiski come in a few hours a week to keep an eye on things and advise the students who work there part-time. Henry Latitiere's students keep the books. The community survey class, led by Jean Comstock and Louis Clark, is planning to write and produce a community newsletter.

Robert Smith is just now explaining a paragraph in a computer manual to Mrs. Broadbent, who listens patiently. She points out that the issue is not what the writer meant but what the text conveys. Smiling, she notes that all people cannot be Robert Smiths; most people struggle on with far less computer knowledge. Robert, who still feels that the description is obvious, is puzzled by Mrs. Broadbent's attack on seemingly competent documentation. He is, however, beginning to get a sense that his technical skills are far better than average.

He looks forward to going down to the shop and working on his bench without the complexities of Mrs. Broadbent's analysis intruding into his daily work of getting the machines to function. He rises and goes to his math class.

Augustus Heinrich Uhlaut is sitting at the back of the pizza shop with firm eye but unsteady hand. He has not fully recovered from the stroke that caused him to close the shop. Gus used to say that he had pizza in his blood from his Italian mother, and he had run the pizza shop for twelve years until his stroke. He then approached Dorothy McClellan about supplying part-time help to run the shop. She wanted a larger role for the school and suggested that students take on bookkeeping, marketing, and some supervisory responsibility as well.

Gus, who could no longer do all this himself, reluctantly agreed. So far it has worked out well, and business is better than ever.

The pizza shop is adjacent to the school cafeteria, which at 11 A.M. is now open. The pizza is available to both the public and the students. It provides an alternative to the mashed potatoes, peas, and rather gray meat that are offered as primary fare. At the other end of the cafeteria (and the food spectrum) is the doughnut counter. All doughnuts there are $.35. This is a project of the special education class and is a major interest of the history teacher, Louis Clark. He suggested that the mentally disabled students could have a wage-earning role in the school community. Furthermore, they would benefit from an environment that was active socially and gave them considerable interpersonal contact. Their world, in the past, protected them almost too much.

A case in point is Oscar "Skippy" Stein. His presence in the school was the result of much difficult maneuvering. As mainstreaming finally became a reality, Skippy found a niche academically and is now moving slowly along in his subjects. His greatest pleasure, though, is the hour he spends selling doughnuts to students in the cafeteria. He likes the greetings, enjoys the bantering, and finds that using the chart he was given by the business students makes giving change an operation that he can do accurately. He would still like to learn to add up the numbers at the end of the day and be able to write them down. Yet he recognizes that some patience is needed, so he smiles and greets his regular customers as any good businessperson should.

Leo Kaminiski has sent an emergency e-mail to Al: the network the print shop uses to collect and return jobs has gone down. Font & Chase's Crystal Lake customer base was too small for survival, so the marketing class developed the strategy of a remote network that permits companies to send data electronically and receive the final output at their own facility. Students wrote a business plan that persuaded a local bank to lend the Crystal Lake High School Enterprise Foundation $20,000 to buy the necessary equipment. Al's e-mail reply is noncommittal: he has a lot of pressing work for Robert at the repair shop but will send him as soon as possible. This delay frustrates the students at the shop, and they decide to call Glenda Barry. She is not available, which frustrates them even more.

Glenda is currently listening to a presentation by students in the advanced chemistry class. One student has analyzed the ecological effect of using salt and sand as winter deicers. Glenda is particularly pleased that the advanced students have found an active role in the new school concept and that they are using their knowledge and analytical skills to serve the community. Such skills are very often left dormant in a traditional high school environment. In Crystal Lake, these students act as the research consultants for the mayor and council. For example, one team of students did a statistical critique of a state report that put Crystal Lake's future in jeopardy with a recommendation to reduce state funding in a number of areas. When the students demonstrated that the evidence did not support the conclusion statistically, the state reinstated a grant of $105,000 that was to have been denied to Crystal Lake. Dorothy McClellan was pleased at that student activity, because it allayed her concern that the better students might be left out of the school, becoming victims of reverse discrimination.

Gus Uhlaut is irritated that his stroke prevents him from showing how to spin a large pizza crust — a skill that he always felt was the mark of a true pizza parlor as well as a great attraction to the customers. One of the marketing students finds this idea intriguing and is seeking someone to train them in the art of pizza spinning. The home economics class has a nutritional watch on the pizza parlor today; this is a monitoring and auditing program to determine if the nutritional value of the food meets the students' daily needs. It is not in the interest of the SBE program to further undermine the already dubious nutritional habits of the students, after all.

Robert Smith has finished math and is relieved to go to Al's Circuit Center. Al tells him to get over to the print shop right away. He has decided it is best to use every opportunity to send the reticent Robert out on calls, because Robert needs to develop his confidence in communicating with people. Al himself had prodded Robert to ask Henry Latitiere to suggest someone from the marketing program who could work with him on customer-service skills. Henry recommended Jennifer Taylor, who happens to be at the print shop when Robert arrives. She suggests they talk later about setting up some objectives for Robert, who tries to put her off. He wants to find out what the problem is with the print shop's communications system, and he finds Jennifer's style intrusive and somewhat threatening. If it were not for his growing realization that his work with Al depends on his personal skills as well as his technical skills, he would rebuff Jennifer completely. Reluctantly, he agrees to a meeting.

Jennifer makes a note in her journal about the meeting time, Robert's resistance, and what she might do about it. (She thinks, but does not write, that Robert is kind of cute.) This journal is one of the means by which she can receive course credit from the several teachers with whom she has independent study contracts. Jennifer is in a program in which she carries out a series of projects. She has contracted to spend a minimum number of hours and produce certain outcomes, including reports on the sales by the print shop and now her customer-service coaching with Robert. This program gives Jennifer a huge range of flexibility; she is not bound by the traditional school, which she found confining. There are now seven students in this program structure. Dorothy McClellan sees it as a prototype for the high school of the future, though she recognizes that many educators and parents still do not accept this concept of a school without classrooms.

Louis Clark is walking downtown with a group of six students, all carrying disposable cameras as part of his photographic history class. His emphasis is on capturing the community on film, not training students in photographic techniques. These photographs, with accompanying narratives that the students will write, will go into an archive that illustrates the path traveled by Crystal Lake.

Jean Comstock has developed a method for using oral histories as part of a needs analysis for the community. She builds on the history classes of Louis Clark and the marketing analysis of Henry Latitiere. Two students have recently gone back and read over the 106 interviews conducted in the past three years. They have noticed a more positive tone in the most recent interviews, maybe indicating that the interview project itself has improved the outlook of Crystal Lake's older residents.

Robert Smith is now back at Al's Circuit Center. His work there is interrupted again when Dorothy McClellan comes to visit him with a member of the adjoining state's education department. This official is interested in the relative impact of in-school enterprise compared to outside apprenticeship. His day in Crystal Lake has confronted him with a range of possibilities: the in-school doughnut business, the pizza shop running as a joint venture between the school and a private owner, the student-operated print shop owned by the Crystal Lake High School Enterprise Foundation, and now Al's Circuit Center, spawned by the school to become an independent business.

It is time for Al to close the shop and drive Robert home. Robert enjoys this part of the day, because Al is about the only person with whom he actually likes to talk. Al's car takes a while to start, and they both agree that an electronic ignition would be an advantage. Al is musing about there being a market for the tuning and repair of modern vehicles that have such a large number of microcomputers and advanced circuitry. Robert wonders if Mrs. Broadbent might help him write something about that. He mentions to Al that he should talk to Henry Latitiere about a marketing survey to find out if there is the business to warrant such an effort. They both have come to take it for granted that the high school can and will provide help in developing their business to meet local needs. Al and Robert could not now imagine that school, work, and community would be anything but a unified system.

9

A Strategy
for Expansion

Most of the activities being conducted by the fictitious students, teachers, and administrators at Veblen and Crystal Lake high schools are similar to activities we saw at the real schools described in the preceding chapters. However, none of the actual sites had developed school-based enterprise to the extent that our imaginary schools have. To move school-based enterprise from its current status as an interesting but marginal set of projects to an organizing principle for the entire high school requires a new vision of education and work, an investment in teachers and curriculum, a set of flexible administrative arrangements, and a rigorous procedure for ongoing evaluation.

A new vision of education and work would make education less egocentric and work less coercive. Education is currently seen as benefiting the student primarily, while production provides for others. Although we may think of education ideally as a process for transmitting a shared cultural heritage, schools in practice are thoroughly individualistic in their treatment of students. Grades are awarded for individual performance; students' explicit goal is to increase their own individual skill, knowledge, and understanding; students pass as individuals from one grade level to the next, and from high school to college. As organized in schools, education is an individual affair.

Work, by contrast, must produce goods or services that other people want. No one is economically self-sufficient; we must all rely on other people to provide at least some of what we need. Although we may sometimes think of work as a means to obtain individual paychecks, the fact is that wages and salaries are paid only because there are customers or clients who benefit from the wage earner's effort. Work is a social transaction.

Combining production with education changes both. When students engage in productive activity, their learning becomes part of a social exchange, benefiting other people as well as themselves. Education becomes less egocentric. It also becomes less abstract, as the consequences of students' actions become more immediate. This can provide new motivation for students in American high schools, where existing incentives have been especially ineffective for the non-college-bound (Bishop, 1989; Rosenbaum, 1989). Even students who are competing for admission to selective four-year colleges can benefit from placing education in a practical context, because information and thought processes acquired in the context of problem solving that has a social purpose are more likely to be remembered and available for application to future problems (Resnick, 1987a, 1987b; Raizen, 1989; Brown, Collins, and Duguid, 1989).

Combining education with production also changes the meaning of work. When productive activity is designed to promote learning, it gives students the experience of work that contributes to their own development. This is in strong contrast to the repetitive, unchallenging jobs available to most students after school and during the summer (Greenberger and Steinberg, 1986). Participation in a setting where productive activity is organized for educational purposes enables students to see how work can be used as a learning experience. This should be useful preparation for an economy in which continued learning at work will increasingly be expected not only of professional and managerial workers but of production and clerical workers as well (Berryman and Bailey, 1992; Marshall and Tucker, 1992). Continued learning includes both acquiring knowledge from other people who already possess it and contributing one's own new ideas. As economic competition increasingly depends on continuous improvement in product design and production methods, motivation at work must depend more on human curiosity and less on fear of economic insecurity.

Recognizing the importance of learning through work does not mean deemphasizing traditional high school subject-matter disciplines — mathematics, English, history, physics, biology, foreign languages, and the rest — if the objective is for students to understand these subjects in depth and in context (as do, for example, students at Thomas Jefferson High School of Science and Technology). The National Council of Teachers of Mathematics (1989) and other subject-specific teacher groups have endorsed this approach.

However, spending time on productive projects may well imply that subjects are covered in less breadth. This might not be a great loss if broad coverage results only in the accumulation of what Whitehead ([1929] 1949) termed "inert facts," fostering what a teacher at Mt. Edgecumbe High School disdainfully called "the Trivial Pursuit type of student." In this view, the fact that broad coverage might help college-bound students obtain higher scores on college admission tests implies only that the current college admission tests should be changed. Yet there might also be other, legitimate reasons to expose students superficially to certain knowledge and ideas. We cannot dismiss the value of breadth entirely. The important thing is to adopt evaluation procedures that measure the relative advantages and disadvantages of school-based enterprise compared to other modes of learning.

Putting the SBE philosophy into more widespread practice will require an investment in teachers and curriculum. Under the influence of contemporary cognitive science, researchers have begun to identify teaching methods that promote learning through "authentic" or "situated" problem solving (Berryman, 1992; Stasz and others, 1993). This is sometimes called cognitive apprenticeship. REAL Enterprises and the Foxfire network are developing curriculum and teaching methods for SBEs. Jobs for the Future, a not-for-profit organization that has been in the forefront of efforts to promote youth apprenticeship, is cultivating methods of work-based learning. The Center for Law and Education, a not-for-profit organization that has advocated teaching "all aspects of the industry," has also been working with teachers to formulate methods that could be used in SBEs.

What is missing is an organizing mechanism that would combine these and other separate efforts into a cohesive initiative that would involve teachers simultaneously in producing curriculum and developing teaching methods for school-based enterprise. An example of such a mechanism is the Mini-Enterprises in Schools Project in Great Britain, which produced curriculum packages and sponsored teacher education during the late 1980s and early 1990s. It would also be useful for both new and experienced teachers in nonvocational subjects to spend some time in work settings outside schools, probably during the summer, on stipends. Funds to support this range of activities in the United States might be found in existing and anticipated budgets for vocational education program improvement, school-to-work transition, career academies, and youth apprenticeship programs.

It is possible for these development activities to recoup some of their costs. Curriculum materials can be sold, for example, and fees can be charged for in-service professional development and technical assistance. The Bay Area Writing Project, which grew into the National Writing Project, is the first and probably best-known example of how a network of teachers teaching teachers can pay some of its own costs by charging for materials and services. Other networks have since emulated the writing teachers. What could be more appropriate than SBE teachers creating a network that includes revenue-generating enterprise?

At the school level, operating an enterprise requires administrative flexibility. Special accounts often must be established for SBE transactions, for example, and some funds may have to be carried forward from one fiscal year to the next. Some SBEs may operate during the summer. Class periods longer than fifty or sixty minutes may be wanted in some programs. Experts from industry might be hired as part-time adjunct instruc-

tors. Special scheduling or credit arrangements for students may
be necessary. Insurance contracts may have to be amended to
cover product liability or workers' compensation. And this is
only a partial list of the administrative issues associated with
school-based enterprise.

A freestanding not-for-profit corporation or foundation
can be established to give the school administration additional
flexibility, as in Fairfax County. State laws might be written
to provide a legal template for such entities. New laws could
also supply explicit enabling language for local school authorities to make arrangements necessary for SBEs. In states where
current law requires any profit from school operations to be
deducted from state aid, SBEs could be exempted.

There are also many ways in which school-based enterprise could be promoted by new policy at the federal level. The
law on vocational education could finally recognize school-based
enterprise as an instructional method, for example. For decades
this law has sanctioned cooperative education, which is another
approach to combining education and work. The same law could
give localities the option to include the estimated market value
of SBE products and services in the performance measures that
are now required for all federally supported vocational education. The Higher Education Act, which has provided special
support for cooperative education, could also begin to acknowl-
edge and support school-based enterprise.

The current policy developments that seem likely to have
the most profound effects on existing and potential SBEs are
the new educational standards and student learning assessments
that are being formulated by the federal and state governments.
If these standards and assessments are limited to students' ability to recall broad knowledge in standard academic subjects,
it will become more difficult to justify devoting students' time
to integrative, in-depth projects, and school-based enterprise will
be doomed. On the other hand, school-based enterprise will become more legitimate if the new standards and assessments emphasize education as Whitehead defined it: the art of the utili-
zation of knowledge. This includes formulating and testing
solutions to real problems, identifying the information needed

in particular situations, combining the abilities and knowledge possessed by different team members, and other generic mental capacities.

Evaluation is essential. Our observations and testimonial evidence suggest that SBEs can strengthen students' intellectual powers while delivering economic and social benefits, but we do not suppose that these outcomes are guaranteed. Any local, state, or federal initiatives to promote school-based enterprise should require ongoing evaluation. Measuring actual outcomes will help enhance the effectiveness of each separate enterprise. It will also begin to take advantage of the opportunity presented by the whole SBE movement: to discover how best to organize productive activity for the purpose of learning.

REFERENCES

Bailey, T. "Can Youth Apprenticeship Thrive in the United States?" *Educational Researcher,* 1993, *22*(3), 4–10.

Berryman, S. E. "Apprenticeship as a Paradigm for Learning." In J. E. Rosenbaum and others, *Youth Apprenticeship in America: Guidelines for Building an Effective System.* Washington, D.C.: William T. Grant Foundation Commission on Youth and America's Future, 1992.

Berryman, S. E., and Bailey, T. *The Double Helix: Education and the Economy.* New York: Teachers College Press, 1992.

Bishop, J. "Why the Apathy in American High Schools?" *Educational Researcher,* 1989, *18*(1), 6–10.

Brown, J. S., Collins, A., and Duguid, P. "Situated Cognition and the Culture of Learning." *Educational Researcher,* 1989, *18*(1), 32–41.

Fidler, J. E. "Law Review Operations and Management." *Journal of Legal Education,* 1983, *33,* 48–63.

Greenberger, E., and Steinberg, L. D. *When Teenagers Work.* New York: Basic Books, 1986.

Jamieson, I., Miller, A., and Watts, A. G. *Mirrors of Work: Work Simulations in Schools.* Philadelphia: Falmer Press, 1988.

Lave, J., and Wenger, E. *Situated Learning: Legitimate Peripheral Participation.* Cambridge, England: Cambridge University Press, 1991.

Manpower Demonstration Research Corporation. *Summary and Findings of the National Supported Work Demonstration.* New York: Ballinger, 1980.

Marshall, R., and Tucker, M. *Thinking for a Living.* New York: Basic Books, 1992.

Mullenax, P. B. "Education for Rural Development. FUNDAEC: A Case Study." Unpublished doctoral dissertation, Department of Educational Administration and Supervision, Bowling Green State University, Ohio, 1982.

Mullinax, M. F., and others. "Labour, Learning, and Service in Five American Colleges." *Education with Production,* 1991, *7*(2), 83–104.

National Council of Teachers of Mathematics, Commission on Standards for School Mathematics. *Curriculum and Evaluation Standards for School Mathematics.* Reston, Va.: National Council of Teachers of Mathematics, 1989.

OECD. *Environment, Schools, and Active Learning.* Paris: Organization for Economic Co-operation and Development, 1991.

Olson, L. "Creating Apprenticeship System Will Be Tough, Advocates Admit." *Education Week,* Mar. 3, 1993a, pp. 1, 29.

Olson, L. "Progressive-Era Concept Now Breaks Mold: NASDC Schools Explore 'Project Learning.'" *Education Week,* Feb. 17, 1993b, pp. 6–7.

Peck, E. "Labour for Education: Berea College." *Education with Production,* 1989, *6*(2), 5–28.

Raizen, S. A. *Reforming Education for Work: A Cognitive Science Perspective.* Berkeley: National Center for Research in Vocational Education, University of California, 1989.

The REAL Story. Newsletter of REAL (Rural Entrepreneurship Through Action Learning), Chapel Hill, North Carolina.

Resnick, L. B. *Education and Learning to Think.* Washington, D.C.: National Academy Press, 1987a.

Resnick, L. B. "Learning In School and Out." *Educational Researcher,* 1987b, *16*, 13–20.

Riggs, R. E. "The Law Review Experience: The Participant View." *Journal of Legal Education,* 1981, *31*, 646–656.

Rosenbaum, J. E. "Empowering Schools and Teachers: A New Link to Jobs for the Non–College Bound." In U.S. Department of Labor, Commission on Workforce Quality and Labor Market Efficiency, *Investing in People: A Strategy to Address America's Workforce Crisis.* Background Papers. Vol. 1. Washington, D.C.: U.S. Department of Labor, 1989.

Sher, J. P. (ed.). *Education in Rural America: A Reassessment of Conventional Wisdom.* Boulder, Colo.: Westview, 1977.

Stasz, C., and others. *Classrooms That Work: Teaching Generic Skills in Academic and Vocational Settings.* Berkeley: National Center for Research in Vocational Education, University of California, 1993.

Steinberg, L., Fegley, S., and Dornbusch, S. M. "Negative Impact of Part-Time Work on Adolescent Adjustment: Evidence from a Longitudinal Study." *Developmental Psychology,* 1993, *29*(2), forthcoming.

Stern, D. "School-Based Enterprise and the Quality of Work Experience: A Study of High School Students." *Youth & Society,* 1984, *15*(4), 401–427.

Stern, D. "Institutions and Incentives for Developing Work-Related Knowledge and Skill." In P. Adler (ed.), *Technology and the Future of Work.* New York: Oxford University Press, 1992a.

Stern, D. *School-to-Work Programs and Services in Secondary Schools and Two-Year Public Postsecondary Institutions: Findings from the National Assessment of Vocational Education Survey.* Berkeley: School of Education, University of California, 1992b.

Stern, D., Stone, J. R., III, Hopkins, C., and McMillion, M. "Quality of Students' Work Experience and Orientation Toward Work." *Youth & Society,* 1990, *22*(2), 263–282.

Stone, J. R., III. "School-Based Enterprise." Paper presented at the annual meeting of the American Vocational Association, 1989.

U.S. Congress. Carl D. Perkins Vocational and Applied Technology Education Act Amendments of 1990. 101st Congress, 2nd session, 1990.

U.S. Department of Labor, Bureau of Labor-Management Relations. *Exploratory Investigations of Pay-for-Knowledge Systems.* BLMR 108. Washington, D.C.: U.S. Department of Labor, 1988.

U.S. Department of Labor, Secretary's Commission on Achieving Necessary Skills (SCANS). *What Work Requires of Schools.* Washington, D.C.: U.S. Department of Labor, 1991.

van Rensburg, P. *Report from Swaneng Hill.* Stockholm, Sweden: Almqvist and Wiksell, 1974.

von Borstel, F. "Productive Education: A Comparative Study of the Present Day Experience in Developing Nations." Unpublished doctoral dissertation, Department of Educational Theory, University of Toronto, Canada, 1982.

Whitehead, A. N. *The Aims of Education.* New York: Mentor Books, 1949. (Originally published 1929.)

Wigginton, E. *Sometimes a Shining Moment: The Foxfire Experience.* New York: Doubleday, 1986.

Williams, P. *The Enterprising Classroom.* Coventry, England: Mini-Enterprise in Schools Project/School Curriculum Industry Partnership, Centre for Education and Industry, University of Warwick, 1991.

INDEX

215

economic benefits of, 92–95, 99; as enterprise, 30–31; operating, 142, 144, 171; starting, 120
Foundation for Applied Technical/Vocational Education: and cost recovery, 82, 86; for enterprises, 18, 19, 20, 22; and networking, 161, 167, 168; and partnerships, 169, 170–171, 173
4-H, 42
Fourier, C., 7
Foxfire, 8, 133, 179, 206
France, enterprises in, 6–7
FUNDAEC Rural University, 9
Future Farmers of America (FFA), 36–37, 113

G

Gateway Technical College: as case-study site, 44–45; price setting by, 124; and quality, 108–109; teachers for, 127
Georgia. *See* Brooks County High School
Gorky Colony, 6
Greenberger, E., 111, 205

H

Habitat for Humanity: and conflicting demands, 158; and networking, 165, 166; and partnerships, 35, 169, 171, 173
Haldeman, T., 190, 191
Hardware/lumberyard project: economic benefits of, 83, 91–92; as enterprise, 25–26; operating, 155, 161–162; starting, 120, 121, 124
High School of Cooperative and Technical Education. *See* Coop Tech
High schools: comprehensive, 17–31; mythical, 183–203; vocational, 32–37
Higher Education Act, 208
Hocking Technical College: Beaver Industries at, 85; as case-study site, 17, 42–44; and community economic development, 95–98;

conflicting demands on, 156; cost recovery at, 82, 83–85; Hocking Special-Ts at, 85–86; industry-wide learning at, 58; integrated learning at, 57; and model workplace, 99–100; National Park Ranger Training Institute at, 83–84; networking by, 163–164; Ohio Technology Transfer Organization (OTTO) at, 43, 96–97; partnerships for, 179; problem solving at, 65–66; quality at, 105–106; subject matter learning at, 50; Wildlife Products at, 43–44; work skills at, 75–76, 78, 79
Hollywood Diner: as case-study site, 38–40; conflicting demands on, 150, 154, 155, 157–158, 159–160; networking by, 161, 164, 165, 166–167; partnerships for, 168–169, 171, 175–177, 179–180; and student independence, 134
Honeywell Research, networking with, 167
Hopkins, C., 10
Horticulture program: applied learning in, 56; as enterprise, 35, 179
Hospitality program: economic benefits of, 84, 85, 99–100; as enterprise, 43; operating, 156

I

Industry, learning multiple aspects of, 58–64
Insurance, and partnerships, 169–170, 185–186

J

Jamaica: enterprise in, 42; teaching in, 44
Jamieson, I., 8
Japan, marketing to, 30–31, 54, 62–63, 94, 171
Jobs: nonschool, and enterprises, 10–15; rotation of, 59–60, 61, 144, 156
Jobs for the Future, 206–207